HOW TO SUCCEED AND MAKE MONEY WITH YOUR FIRST RENTAL HOUSE

Douglas A. Keipper

and

Sean M. Lyden

WILEY

John Wiley & Sons, Inc.

Published by John Wiley & Sons, Inc., Hoboken, New Jersey.
Published simultaneously in Canada.

For general information on our other products and services please contact our Customer Care Department within the United States at (800) 762-2974, outside the United States at (317) 572-3993 or fax (317) 572-4002.

Wiley also publishes its books in a variety of electronic formats. Some content that appears in print may not be available in electronic books. For more information about Wiley products, visit our web site at www.wiley.com.

The author is not an attorney or a CPA and does not intend to give legal or tax advice. You should seek competent advice from lawyers and CPAs.

Library of Congress Cataloging-in-Publication Data:
Keipper, Douglas, 1962–
    How to succeed and make money with your first rental house / Douglas Keipper
and Sean Lyden
        p.   cm.
    Includes index.
    ISBN 0-471-45140-1 (pbk. : alk. paper)
    1. Real estate investment—United States.   2. Real estate investment—United
States—Finance.   3. Rental housing—United States.   4. Real estate
management—United States.   I. Lyden, Sean, 1972–   II. Title.
HD255.K372004
333.33'85'0973—dc21   2003049735

Printed in the United States of America.

10 9 8 7 6 5 4 3 2 1

This book was not possible without the loving support and co-borrower signature of my wife Nan and my children Rebecca and Rachel, who may not understand why "Daddy bought a rental house" until they go to college—with the proceeds. I must thank my mother, who typed my dictation and my father, who encouraged me all the way. A special thanks to my brothers, sister, in-laws, and friends who never laughed in my face at either buying a rental house or writing a book. Having good supportive friends and family is worth more than money. And to Sean, who battled his own set of circumstances during the writing of this book and never gave up—even when I wanted to. I would also like to thank Mike Hamilton at John Wiley & Sons for taking my book proposal seriously and for giving me the opportunity to share my experience—my intellectual sister still can't believe it.

—Doug Keipper
www.firstrentalhouse.com

I dedicate this book to my beautiful bride Jennifer and our precious daughters, Adair and Meleah, who've been more than patient and loving toward me during the long hours devoted to this project. Furthermore, I'm grateful to Doug Keipper for the privilege to team up with him on this book. Doug's experiences, courage, and optimism motivate me to succeed in my own real estate endeavors!

—Sean Lyden

CONTENTS

Chapter 1

Seize the Opportunity!   **1**
  My Story   2
  $9,000 Cash Back at Closing   5
  Sleepless Nights   6
  Creating Your Own Success Story   7
  Do You Have the Right Stuff?   10
  Action Step   14
  Motivational Quotes   14

Chapter 2

Leveraging OPM—Other People's Money!   **15**
  Bigger Rates of Return   15
  Where to Get the Money   16

Chapter 3

Building a Winning Project Team   **31**
  Mentors   32
  The Banker or Mortgage Lender   37
  The Real Estate Agent   38

CONTENTS

Attorneys   41
Accountants   43
Contractors   43
Motivational Quote   47

Chapter 4

Getting over the Hump   **49**
Action Step   61
Motivational Quotes   61

Chapter 5

Getting the Government to Pay Your Rent!   **63**
How Does Section 8 Work?   64
Does Your House Qualify?   66
How Do You Participate?   71
What Are Your Responsibilities as a Section 8 Landlord?   71
Motivational Quote   73

Chapter 6

Finding the Right House   **75**
Become an Expert on Location   78
Other Considerations   82
Analyze the Cash-Flow Opportunity   84
Summary   90
Home Inspections   91
Houses We Did Not Buy and Why   94
Motivational Quotes   98

Chapter 7

A House versus a Home   **99**
The Difference between a House and a Home   99
Motivational Quotes   114

Contents

Chapter 8

Show Me the Money!   **115**
   Where the Money Came from to Buy My First
     Rental House   115
   Rental House Points versus Primary House Points   122
   Private Mortgage Insurance   123
   The Bottom Line   124

Chapter 9

Welcome to the Closing Table!   **127**
   RESPA Required Disclosures   129

Chapter 10

Rehabbing Your Rental House   **133**
   Taking Stock   133
   The First Saturday   134
   The Second Saturday   136
   The Third Saturday   138
   The Fourth Saturday   139
   The Fifth Saturday   140
   The Sixth Saturday   141
   The Seventh Saturday   142
   Monday Morning Quarterback   144
   Getting the Most Bang for Your Renovation Buck   145
   Motivational Quotes   149

Chapter 11

How I Landed a Tenant   **151**
   Marketing, Marketing, Marketing   152
   Showing the House   155
   When the Right Guy Showed Up—My First Tenant   157
   Motivational Quote   159

CONTENTS

Chapter 12

Qualifying a Tenant   **161**
- Why Is It Necessary?   161
- What Am I Looking for?   162
- The Credit Report   163
- Renter Profiles   166
- Verify the Funds   168
- Inspection   169

Chapter 13

Protecting Your Investment with the Right Lease Agreements   **171**
- What Makes a Good Lease Agreement?   171
- Where Do You Find Lease Agreements?   176

Chapter 14

What to Expect When Becoming a Landlord   **181**
- Motivational Quote   187

Chapter 15

Timeline   **189**

Chapter 16

Getting Paid on Time   **197**
- How Eviction Works   198
- Do Not Make These Landlord Mistakes   201
- Resources for Additional Information   202
- Final Thoughts from the Author   202
- Motivational Quote   202

Appendix of Selected Mortgage Terms   *203*

Bibliography   *221*

Index   *223*

CHAPTER 1

Seize the Opportunity!

If you've been looking to make money in real estate, whether part-time or full-time, you've probably seen the 2 A.M. infomercials that promise: "Earn unlimited income in your spare time!" "Create a personal fortune in real estate with *no money down!*" "Only $75 will bring you hundreds of thousands of dollars in real estate earnings!!!" These infomercials make buying and managing rental properties seem so easy. They depict people just like you and me enjoying luxury cars, boats, and huge homes—and all the leisure time in the world.

Does this sound too good to be true? Well, yes and no. Can you make a lot of money in rental properties and retire rich? Absolutely! Many people have done so. But, is it instant and easy money? Not necessarily. Just as in any business, to make money in real estate you must work hard and be disciplined, persistent, and educated. *Then* you'll experience the fruit of your labor. The reality is that the process of buying a rental house—especially your first one—isn't as easy as it may seem on TV. But one thing is for sure: Buying rental property can be a lot of fun, very profitable, and personally fulfilling when you have the right expectations and are willing to work hard to succeed at it! And to increase your chance of success you need to be educated.

And that's what this book is about. It's designed to show you how to make buying your first rental house a success, from my personal experience. I'll share how I bought my first rental house—the challenges and fears I faced, the people I needed to meet, the books I read, what I did right (and what I did wrong), and what I will do differently on the next one. Remember when you were a kid how your parents would tell you about what happened when they were young? Well, they didn't want you to make the same mistakes they did. They wanted you to learn from their experiences. I want you to learn from my experiences. To give you a frame of reference, for my first rental house, after working 8 to 12 hours for seven straight Saturdays, I earned back my down payment and rehab costs and then cashed out $9,000 tax-free on top of all that. Pretty cool, huh? Well, if a 2.7 GPA from Ball State University can do this, so can you. And this book will show you how!

MY STORY

Here's my situation. I am 40 years old, a college graduate, and the youngest of four children. I've been in various facets of the financial services industry for more than 12 years, starting in mortgage banking, retail banking, financial planning, and now settling in as a commercial banker. Granted, I may have more financial training than most readers, but I also have more than most real estate investors who are worth 10 times as much as I am. So being a financial expert is obviously not the magic ingredient to getting started. It is not necessary to have an extensive financial background. This book will discuss many of the financial ins and outs and details of what you can expect. I'm married with two daughters, eight and six years old, and see buying rental properties as a means to diversify my income, pay for my daughters' college educations (and weddings, of course!), and for my wife and me to retire comfortably. Buying my first rental house is the first step to achieving these goals.

I first got interested in real estate when my older brother Phil read *Nothing Down* by Robert G. Allen (Simon & Schuster) back in the early to mid 1980s. I was probably a freshman in college and he was a fifth-year architecture major. A few years later he confided to me that he spent an hour a day thinking about how to make money without having to work every day. Eventually he was in a commercial real estate deal with seven partners that turned out great, but he has not gone further than that one deal. Even though he never pursued additional deals, I was fascinated by the details of that one major project.

Phil is so conservative by nature that the concept of working for profits rather than wages has always scared him. I, on the other hand, have always been fascinated by working for profits rather than wages. I saw my father get laid off after 37 years with the same company because a new accountant thought he was overpaid. As you might imagine, my father is not a big fan of accountants. Working for wages doesn't provide *real* security. It provides the *illusion* of security. Real security lies between your ears. Real security comes from having several streams of income through several types of skills. You could have been the best railroad engineer in the world, but when the airplane came along you would be out of a job. Or you could be the best airline pilot in the world, with 25 years' experience, and then videoconferencing and terrorism come along and you get laid off. The world is constantly evolving. Either change and adapt or get left behind. The choice is yours.

I had seen some of my friends make money in real estate, and in the spring of 2002 I decided it was time for me to do it. I thought, "Why not? I have above-average skills in carpentry and home repair.

I finished my basement in 1996. I was a mechanic through high school and college at a marina where I obviously worked with my hands every day. I have a brother who is an architect. I used to have a neighbor who was a building superintendent. Heck! I can ask a lot of questions at Home Depot and Lowe's and get all the free advice I need! While finishing my basement, I visited the home supply stores often. If I was venturing into an area I had never worked in before, I would ask two or three different store employees the same question. Then I might also ask a friend or neighbor. When I received a consistent answer, I would go with that solution. I have also been collecting business cards of people who could help me with electrical and plumbing work, as I need it. So what's holding me back?" The only answer was looking at me in the mirror, and he was not getting any younger.

Are you reading this and thinking, "Doug, I don't even own a hammer, and I don't have a clue how to open a paint can"? Fret not! I did not do all the work myself. Although I can do some electrical work and plumbing, I preferred to leave all that to the experts. My wife was not too keen on having me on the roof, either. So we had help there also. I will discuss in detail later in the book how to develop your professional team.

Where most people think of excuses as to why they can *not* do something, I began listing all the reasons why I *can*. I knew the mortgage business. I knew how to fix toilets, patch drywall, and light the pilot light on a hot water heater (why don't they call it a cold water heater?). I had all the hand tools of an average homeowner (well, maybe a few more tools than the *average* homeowner).

You see, often the biggest obstacles that keep people from succeeding in the real estate business are the obstacles they erect in their own minds—the fears, apprehensions, and worries that come with making a significant change (for the better) in your life. It was time I worked on the obstacles holding me back. Therefore, your first homework assignment is to make an "I can" list. Hint: Your first reason should be "If Doug can do it, I can, too!"

$9,000 CASH BACK AT CLOSING

What I did with this first house is a textbook case on the "cash back at closing" type of deal. I'll go in more detail on this in Chapter 8, but here's the overview. The house was foreclosed, vacant, and now owned by a bank. It was dirty inside and outside. The split-level house was appraised for $122,000, and I bought it for $101,000. I got the bank to finance 80 percent of the appraised value, which is $97,600, for the first mortgage. I kicked in $3,400 as a down payment to cover the difference. I then spent $3,000 on expenses such as utilities, a mortgage payment, application fee, appraisal, insurance, and so forth. I spent $7,000 at Home Depot and Lowe's and with contractors to do all the repairs and then advertised it for rent.

Once I fixed up the house, it was appraised for $139,000. I got a new mortgage for 90 percent of the appraised value, or $125,000. So here's how the numbers break down:

- $125,000—new mortgage.
- $97,600—pay off initial mortgage.
- $7,000—to cover expenses (Home Depot, Lowe's, contractors, newspaper ads).
- $5,000—for refinancing expenses, including two points for investor rates.
- $3,000—for expenses (utilities, insurance, mortgage payment, etc.).
- $3,400—for down payment.

The net result? $9,000 to me tax-free. This is because loans are *not* taxable! The money can be spent just like income but it doesn't get taxed like income. All this for seven Saturdays' worth of work! That is an average of $1,285 per day of labor. Of course, that was only the middle of the process. It took time to learn about real estate investing. It took time locating a house. It took time renting out the house. I will take time to maintain the house.

SLEEPLESS NIGHTS

Making money is the fun part. But just as with any worthwhile, moneymaking endeavor, you must be willing to pay the price. For me, the price was enduring several sleepless nights, seven sore Sundays, and time away from home.

Waking up at 2:37 A.M. is not fun, and I did it a lot. I would lie awake worrying whether I was doing the right thing, how much work needed to be done before I could advertise it for rent, and how much more money I would have to spend. What if somebody breaks in and steals all my tools? Did I get the right insurance coverage on the house? How can I get the master bathroom sink to stop dripping? My wife, on the other hand, never lost a minute of sleep! I would tiptoe out of the bedroom wide awake, and very jealous.

Sometimes I sat at my computer and tried to list all the things I had to do to this house to get it ready to rent. I thought if I got it all out of my head that way it would help me to sleep better. It didn't, so save yourself some time and don't try that method. A couple of times I watched Carlton Sheets infomercials and tried to picture myself on his show. I'd find myself getting mad at those people who made it sound easy. Again, don't try that method! I would be so worn out the next day that I'd come home from work, eat dinner, and then fall asleep on the couch with my kids as we watched *Animal Planet*. I've taken Melatonin for years to help me sleep at night, but during this process it didn't seem to help much.

My wife Nan and the kids coped well with Daddy being gone for seven straight Saturdays, 8 to 12 hours at a time. They would always bring lunch, and Nan would try to help for an hour or two before the kids wore out our patience and theirs. If you have ever tried to paint with children around, you know they always want to help. They get a paintbrush, make about five strokes with a brush, and they are done! Now you have an extra paintbrush to clean. Then Nan had to leave with the kids to maintain sanity in the marriage. I will talk later about your support group, but it is worth hearing it here, too. Your family needs to know what is involved.

Now that I am on the other side of things, I sleep a lot better and do not worry as much. Why? I have gone through the process, survived, and now know what to expect as I build my real estate portfolio. You see, the hardest part about getting into real estate investing is buying the *first* property. Once you've gotten over the "first-house jitters," you'll gain more confidence to take your real estate assets—and cash flow—to the next level.

CREATING YOUR OWN SUCCESS STORY

With that said, let's talk about you. What is your story? What has gotten you interested in buying rental properties? What are your goals? What kind of money do you want to make from your own real estate business? What do you want the money to do for you? Are you looking to generate retirement income or save for your child's education or make enough money to vacation anywhere you want in the world? Does that sound like another homework assignment? Well, I will not be checking your homework, but I do think you need clearly defined goals. Have a plan for your profits from your first house. Do you want to pay off a loan? Do you want a down payment for a second rental house? By setting a goal, you will become more focused on what needs to be done to get there.

Whatever your financial goals, investing in rental properties can be a great vehicle for creating your own success story. Why? Consider these trends:

- **Stock market decline.** As of this writing, the Standard & Poor's 500-stock index is down 25 percent over the past 12 months. The Nasdaq 100 is 65 percent below its March 2000 peak. Investors are looking to protect themselves from further losses and have been moving money into hard assets that they can see, smell, and touch—like real estate. Am I advising you to sell your stocks and buy real estate? No! However, these statistics should cause you to think more about diversification.

- **Unsettled job market.** Job security is a myth—and the baby boomers are especially coming to terms with this. The number of unemployed workers age 55 and older has jumped about 23 percent, from 431,000 in June 2000 to 521,000 in June 2001, according to the U.S. Department of Labor. Job hunts for unemployed boomers are taking longer and yielding smaller salaries. According to a recent study cited by *USA Today*, workers over 50 take almost twice as long to identify and get a new professional role than workers who are 30 or younger. The study also found that as workers get older, their salary prospects plateau and eventually decrease. Even workers with relatively safe careers are thinking more about how they would fend for themselves in a major down market.

   Guess what? There is no age discrimination in buying real estate. An 86-year-old person can qualify for a 30-year mortgage. A lender cannot turn someone down simply because of the person's age. Theoretically, we know chances are not good for someone to live to 116 to pay back that loan. However, if the applicant qualifies, the loan will be approved. If the borrower dies, the heirs can sell the house and pay off the loan.

- **Favorable interest rates.** Bankers typically require a little higher interest rate when lending for an investment property. But with 30-year mortgage rates running just above their three-decade low, you can still find financing for about 7 to 8 percent. The neat thing about real estate that you don't get with stocks, bonds, and mutual funds is that the bank will lend you 90 percent of the money to buy a house. This is great leverage! You certainly won't find banks willing to lend you 90 percent of the money to buy mutual fund shares—not even if the fund has a 50-year track record! So what does this say about real estate? The bank is very comfortable with using real estate as collateral because historically it not only has held its value, it appreciates in value.

■ **Tax incentives.** There are three types of income you can earn—and here is the breakdown:

1. *Earned income and dividend income.* This is your salary or commission job with W-2 or 1099 federal taxes up to 39.6 percent plus state taxes (in Georgia it is 6 percent, so there we go up to 45.6 percent total). Don't forget your 14 percent social *in*security tax (FICA).

2. *Long-term capital gains.* This refers to money that is created from selling an asset like a stock that you owned for more than one year—it's generally taxed at 20 percent federal plus state tax. For example: You buy XYZ stock at $10 a share and sell it for $20 two years later. You will be taxed $10 per share profit at 20 percent. That is an after federal tax profit of $8 per share minus your state tax.

3. *Passive income.* This can be money generated from rental houses. With depreciation, tax deductions, and write-offs we can usually get that down to close to 0 percent taxes or at least in the low single digits.

Now . . . where would *you* like to spend your time? Working for an income that is taxed at 45 percent or 0 percent?

■ **Consistent track record.** Over the long term, housing has proved to be a consistent, if unspectacular, performer. According to the government's House Price Index, the average home value in the United States has increased 32 percent in the five years ended March 31, 2002. The government says the average house gained 8.8 percent in value in the 12 months also ending March 31. Rising prices have led to a buildup in home equity that gives many aspiring landlords a source of wealth to tap for a down payment on a rental property. Most of the equity you acquire in your home over a long period of time will come from its appreciation, not from your monthly payments reducing the outstanding principal on the mortgage.

DO YOU HAVE THE RIGHT STUFF?

Do you have what it takes to succeed in rental property investing? By this, I don't mean financial assets like cash and credit. While these are important, what's absolutely essential is having the right psychological makeup, the *intangible* assets to make it. Just as with any great business opportunity, real estate investing is not for everyone. That's because, contrary to popular get-rich-quick gospels, real estate investing requires a lot of hard work and personal sacrifice. You are obviously willing to make a time investment. After all, you bought this book when you could have bought an entertaining Tom Clancy book! Not that this isn't a hotbed of excitement. However, don't wait for the movie.

What are the intangible assets you need to succeed in real estate? Ask yourself these 10 questions.

1. **Can I stomach the risks?** You must overcome your fears of failure as nagging negative thoughts run through your head, like:

   - What if I buy this house, fix it up, and nobody rents it? Okay, is that a realistic worry? You may need to adjust the rent or be creative. But the chances of never renting are slim.
   - What if the house generates *negative* cash flow? How will I keep from losing my shirt? No one recommends negative cash flow, so don't go into a deal that appears to be negative from the beginning. However, if you have a setback, like more repairs than you anticipated, look at the numbers. This is not where you want to be, but don't let the fear of this keep you from pursuing the possibility.
   - What happens if my tenants make two payments and walk out after trashing my property? Yes, this is possible, and if you stay a landlord long enough it may hap-

pen. Do some research of the probability of that happening. Who do you know who is a landlord now? I was amazed to find out how many people in my church and how many of my friends' parents had rental property. Ask them how many times they have had a renter trash the house in two months. If you have enough properties this may eventually happen, but chances are slim it will happen on your first house. That is why we get credit applications on prospective tenants.

- What if my house catches on fire? That is why we have insurance. I would encourage you to meet your property insurance agent for breakfast or lunch and discuss details about what is covered and what is not covered. He/she will have some wonderful insights and might be able to hook you up with a client who could act as a mentor to you.
- What if an eyesore like a gas station is built next door and devalues my property? You can do your part to reduce this risk by doing your homework. Check to make sure there are no rezoning plans for the immediate location around your prospective property. If you buy a house in a subdivision you have drastically reduced that chance.

If you can stomach the risks, you'll do fine. Just make sure you go into a venture with your eyes wide open and make low offers.

2. **Do I have the time to devote to this?** If you travel several days per week and have two small children at home, you may not have time to do this. Count the cost (in time) before you dive in. This way, you're committed to spending whatever time it takes to succeed. If you feel guilty about the time, you will not enjoy the work nearly as much.

3. **Do I have the hunger to keep learning and growing?** Knowledge is literally power. The more you learn about

the business, the more money you'll make—and the less money you'll lose. Do you understand mortgages? Do you like to deal with people? Do you like to work with your hands? Do you know how to paint? Do you know how to fix a toilet? Do you know how to fix a leaky faucet? Do you know how to research problems and find a solution? Identify what you need to learn and then focus your time and resources on acquiring the knowledge and skills you need to overcome the deficiencies. This book, along with others I recommend you read, and your local home improvement store will get you well on your way to knowing what you need to know.

4. **Do I possess an opportunity mentality?** What one person sees as a dump a savvy real estate investor sees as a potential cash cow. You need to see opportunities where others do not. The smell of opportunity is cat urine. When you walk into a house that literally stinks and you can immediately knock $10,000 to $15,000 off the asking price. New carpets and paint might cost $3,500. Cosmetic problems will turn off 99 percent of the people looking at a house. You have to look at this house through rose-colored glasses. See the house as it will be when renovated.

5. **Am I self-motivated?** As motivational guru Zig Ziglar puts it: "If you do the things you *ought* to do *when* you ought to do them, a day will come when you do the things you *want* to do *when* you want to do them." You are the boss on this project. No one is going to watch over your shoulder and encourage you. You must be your own motivation. Get back to that "I can" list and build off of your accomplishments.

6. **Do I have access to financial reserves?** Do you have a savings account, an equity line of credit on your current home, or credit cards for repairs, advertising expenses, and so forth? Don't forget to look beyond your finances to other people's money. What if you do the work but Bob supplies

the money? Having the money is different from having access to the money. You just need the access!

7. **Do I have access to partners?** Who can I call on to help me? Two people going in together on their first deal might have a calming effect on both. They might team up for financial reasons or for simple collaboration. I consider my wife a partner, and she was my sounding board on many occasions.

8. **Am I coachable?** Am I willing to learn, change my habits, and forgive myself for mistakes? I hope you have already begun to learn from this book. As for mistakes, they are only truly mistakes when you don't learn from them. You will read about several changes I would have made to my first success story. I'm not mad at myself for making mistakes—I didn't know any better—and next time there will be fewer regrets. I'm still proud of myself for doing the first deal. To get the first deal behind you is a wonderful feeling. The second rental property will be so much easier—and I bet I make some mistakes there, too!

9. **Am I able to withstand criticism?** What if my family and friends think I've lost my mind—will I be able to stand up to their ridicule? Let me make a suggestion here. If you know family members or friends will not be supportive, then don't tell them. Currently my father-in-law does not know about our rental house. As a child of the Depression, he would have lost sleep for weeks worrying about our debt. That was my job! I didn't need company. What good would come from telling him? Chances are you will find your friends and family to be more supportive than you expected. I had much more support than I expected.

10. **Am I sophisticated and wary?** Will I see at least 10 houses before I put an offer on a house? We all want to put a bid on the first house we look at. Will I resist the temptation to buy something I really don't feel comfortable with? Know the difference between nerves and that old gut feeling.

If you answered "yes" to each of these questions about yourself, you stand a great chance for success. Whether you're looking to become a big-time real estate mogul or simply to earn part-time, supplemental income, this book will show you how to take the first critical steps to make it happen.

ACTION STEP

Log on to my web site at www.firstrentalhouse.com and sign up for my free newsletter. You'll also be able to see my schedule of book signings and seminars.

MOTIVATIONAL QUOTES

Small opportunities are often the beginning of great enterprises.
Demosthenes

A simple man believes anything, but a prudent man gives thought to his steps.
Proverbs 14:15

CHAPTER 2

Leveraging OPM— Other People's Money!

BIGGER RATES OF RETURN

Why is it a good idea to use other people's money when it comes to buying rental property?

Suppose, for example, you buy a $100,000 house with cash and own it free and clear of any mortgage. You have landed a tenant to rent your house for $1,000 per month. Out of that $1,000, you may have to pay $200 a month in taxes, insurance, maintenance reserves, vacancy reserves, and advertising expenses. Therefore, your positive cash flow is $800 per month. So, what's your return on investment? Multiply $800 a month by 12 months, and your positive cash flow for the year is $9,600. Then divide $9,600 by the $100,000 cash you paid to buy the house, and that gives you a 9.6 percent rate of return. Not bad, huh? Compare that return with current certificate of deposit (CD) rates (in 2002 CDs are paying between 2 percent and 3 percent), and it seems that owning the house free and clear gives you a pretty decent return on investment.

But consider what your rate of return would be when you leverage other people's money. Say you bought that same $100,000 home but put only $5,000 down and borrowed the remaining $95,000. And for numbers' sake, suppose your positive cash flow is $100 per month. This number may seem small compared to $800 per month in the preceding example, but the goal here is return on investment. Multiply $100 per month by 12 months, which is $1,200 for the year. Now, here's the magic of OPM. Divide the $1,200 annual cash flow by your $5,000 cash down payment, and you've generated a 24 percent rate of return. And since you put only $5,000 down instead of $100,000, you gain leverage to buy 20 more houses with the same $100,000. Wow!

Let's take a look at the long-term annual appreciation on these two investments. If the value of our one house goes up 3 percent annually and we compound the return, then in 10 years it will have gone from $100,000 to $130,000 in value—a long-term capital gain of $30,000. If we had 20 houses just like that, then we would have 20 times that capital gain or $600,000. Granted we would have more management problems, but in this chapter we're just talking about the benefits of using other people's money.

When you leverage other people's money, you dramatically improve your rates of return on your rental properties and build a much larger, potentially more lucrative portfolio.

WHERE TO GET THE MONEY

Where do you go to get the money? Here are seven places to consider:

1. **Savings and loan.** First of all are savings and loans, also called thrift institutions. Savings and loan associations are the largest lenders of traditional home mortgages. A gov-

ernment cleanup of bad loans of S&Ls in the 1990s left behind the stronger savings and loans. These institutions remain the major source of funding for home mortgage loans. S&Ls are often called savings banks in the eastern part of the United States.

2. **Commercial banks.** Commercial banks offer attractive loan terms, particularly if they evaluate their entire banking relationship with you. Some commercial banks have their own real estate departments and will service your mortgage loan. Other commercial banks sell their mortgages to Fannie Mae and Freddie Mac. These are two major government-sponsored enterprises that specialize in buying residential mortgages from lenders. See appendix of mortgage terms.

3. **Mortgage bankers.** Mortgage bankers borrow money from banks or pools of investors, underwrite the loans, and sell them to investors for a profit. They often receive a fee from these investors for servicing a mortgage. Mortgage servicing includes collecting monthly payments, sending out loan statements, and distributing loan payments to investors. For more information see the web site at the Mortgage Bankers Association of America, www.mbaa.org.

4. **Mortgage brokers.** Mortgage brokers circulate or shop for loan applications among lenders to find the most attractive terms for the borrower. In exchange, the lender pays the broker a fee. My current mortgage broker works for a bank, so I have access to both bank loans and broker loans. I would encourage you to find a similar type of situation.

5. **Homeowners.** You may find that the current homeowner is willing to offer financing in exchange for selling the home sooner. This means that the seller becomes your lender. The common means of financing is for the seller to accept a mortgage note. A mortgage note requires you to make monthly payments to the seller instead of a bank or other lender. Whereas the other loans are easy to find and could be harder to qualify for, this loan is harder to find and could be easier to

qualify for. One advantage is that it doesn't affect your credit score. I will discuss credit scores later in this chapter.

6. **Credit unions.** Since credit unions are owned by their members, they're called cooperative financial institutions. Since they are nonprofit institutions, credit unions may offer attractive mortgage rates to their members. Like commercial mortgage lenders, credit unions sell their loans to Fannie Mae and Freddie Mac. The National Credit Union Administration regulates the credit union industry. It has been my personal experience that credit unions will have far more conservative guidelines in lending money. They will require lower loan-to-value ratios. In other words, they may lend only 70 percent or 80 percent of the appraised value or sales price, whichever is lower. This will result in you having a larger down payment, and as you will read later, I don't like down payments.

7. **Private investors/partners.** If you find the deal of a lifetime (and they can happen almost monthly), and you don't have adequate credit or financing to secure the deal, consider private investors or partners. What if your rich friend/uncle/neighbor had the money or credit but didn't have the time to find the deals? You two could partner up to split the profits! If you have a hard time finding a partner, join a real estate investment club. In Georgia it's called the GaREIA, an acronym for Georgia Real Estate Investors Association. You can find them on the Internet at www.gareia.org. You'll meet plenty of people with good credit and access to money. Try to find someone who has had rental properties for at least five years. You'll probably meet some who have had rental properties for 20 years.

As you seek potential partners, you may run across "hard money lenders." These folks are very high-priced lenders who use your collateral only to determine if they will make the loan. It's kind of like a pawnshop for real estate. The interest rates can go as high as 21 percent. Try to avoid these people. Although technically and legally there is nothing wrong with hard money lenders, their loans are very expensive and thus would cut into your profits. Look for partners instead. Again, like the owner financing, partners will free up your credit to buy more houses.

Credit Reports

We could write an entire book on credit reports. This will be a brief overview of credit reports and creditworthiness. What are your mortgage brokers or bankers looking for to determine if they are going to make your loan?

They are going to look at your collateral for the loan. In this case, that's going to be your house. They determine the value of your house by an appraisal, which usually costs $250 to $300. The highest interest rate loans are those that have no collateral, sometimes called signature loans. These are the riskiest loans to the bank since there is no recourse if you fail to pay.

They are going to look at your ability to repay the loan. In other words, do you make enough money to pay it back? You will not be able to use all the rent on your property as income to qualify for the loan. General lending guidelines allow 75 percent of the income to be applied against the mortgage payment to allow for vacancies advertising, and maintenance. For example, if your rental income is $1,000 per month and your mortgage payment is $1,000 per month, the mortgage company will allow you to use $750 as rental income for qualification purposes. In this scenario you will have to be qualified with a $250 per month payment. After two years of successfully managing rental properties you may find this requirement is not so cut-and-dried—especially if you have some cash reserves.

The are going to look at your willingness to repay the loan. There are many people who make money but are just too lazy or unorganized to pay back their loans in a timely manner. The way banks verify your willingness to repay loans is through your credit report. In the United States there are three major repositories where credit report information is collected. They are Equifax, Experian, and TransUnion. We are going into detail regarding each of those three repositories in just a moment. Your credit report, sometimes referred to as your credit history or credit file, can take personal information gathered from many sources on an ongoing basis. Most companies that have extended you credit will provide information to the three major credit report agencies.

What information is included in your credit report? Here's a breakdown of what you'll find.

Your name and any variations of your name.
Your Social Security number.
Your date of birth.
Previous addresses.
Your current address.
Employment data.
Public records that include liens, bankruptcies, civil judgments, and
  so on.
Inquiries.
Credit accounts and payment history, which will be the largest part
  of your credit report.
Credit score.

Credit Scores

Credit scores allow the lender to look at your credit report without discrimination. A credit score does not know if you are African-American or Caucasian, Asian or Hispanic, male or female, or if you are Catholic, Jewish, Methodist, or Buddhist. It doesn't know if you are on a salary or if you are self-employed. *There is no discrimination in a credit score.* A credit score is a mathematical analysis of your credit and shows the lender the probability of your repayment.

Credit scores generally range from 400 to 800. Higher scores are considered better scores. That is, the higher your score, the more favorably lenders will look on you. If you have a credit score of 720, which is a good score, you are going to have a wider array of loans and credit products available to you with much better terms and rates than if you have a score of 520. Most lenders will consider offering someone with a good score very competitive rates and terms on loan products. Some lenders may require additional information such as income or type of job to more accurately set their guidelines.

Summary of factors affecting your score.   Credit scores are calculated based on the information contained in your credit history.

Positive factors   Here are the top factors that reflect your good credit behavior, listed in priority of impact on your score:

1. There is no evidence of your having seriously late payment behavior.
2. You demonstrate a relatively long credit history.

Negative factors   The top negative factors where you have the most opportunity to take action in order to increase your score over time:

1. You have missed payments reported on your credit accounts. We all have been a couple of days late on making some payments. That will not to appear on your report. Generally, a creditor will report you "late" at 30 days, 60 days, and 90 days.
2. The amount owed on your non-mortgage-related accounts is too high. In other words, if you have very high credit card balances that will negatively affect your credit score.
3. You have a large number of credit cards. This means you have access to a lot of credit. Sometimes that will affect your score. Watching your credit score is very important. You want to avoid opening a large number of unnecessary credit accounts,

like when you go Christmas shopping and they offer you a 10 percent discount to put your new purchases on that store's credit card. Avoid this trap. The credit company is evaluating your potential to spend. If you have six credit cards with $1,000 limits, you could have $6,000 worth of debt the next day. Trust me, I could do that at Home Depot and Circuit City in two hours! Also, you'll create unwanted inquiries into your credit, which can lower your score.

Credit Reporting Agencies

There are three credit repositories in the United States. In the Southeast most creditors are going to report to Equifax as their primary reporting agency. If you live in Georgia and send a car payment to a creditor in California it may not show up on your Equifax credit report. When you get a mortgage, the loan officer or processor may inform you that they are getting a three-file credit report. This means they are getting information from all three agencies.

Equifax. Equifax has been in business for over 100 years, with over 4,800 employees in 12 different countries. You can order your Equifax credit report by phone, by mail, or by Internet. By telephone, the number is 1-800-997-2493. You may also call 1-800-685-1111. The basic fee is $9.00. If you live in one of the following six states you are entitled to a free copy of your Equifax credit report: Georgia, Colorado, New Jersey, Maryland, Massachusetts, and Vermont. You can order your credit report by mail by writing to:

Equifax Consumer Services
Disclosure Department
P.O. Box 740241
Atlanta, GA 30374

Enclose a $9.00 check or money order and include the following information when writing:

Full name, including Jr., Sr., III, IV, etc.
Social Security number.
Current and previous addresses for the past five years.
Date of birth.
Signature.
Contact telephone number.

You may also obtain your Equifax credit report by Internet by going to www.equifax.com. You may dispute inaccuracies on your Equifax credit report by writing to:

Equifax Information Services
P.O. Box 740256
Atlanta, GA 30374

The dispute process can take up to 30 days to be completed.

You can also get a free copy of your credit report if you have been denied credit by phone or mail.

TransUnion.   In the Northeast most creditors will report to Trans-Union. TransUnion has 3,600 employees worldwide and serves all 50 states. You can order a credit report from TransUnion by phone at 1-800-888-4213. You can order it online at www.transunion.com, or you can order by mail at:

TransUnion Consumer Disclosure Center
P.O. Box 1000
Chester, PA 19022

You will need to provide all the same information as requested by Equifax. You also get a free credit report if you live in those same six states as listed for Equifax.

Experian.   West of the Mississippi River most creditors will report to Experian. Experian employs more than 6,600 people in North

America and is headquartered in Costa Mesa, California, with operations throughout the United States and 12 other countries. Order your Experian credit report by calling toll free 1-888-397-3742, or you can order through its web site at www.Experian.com.

Credit Problems

You should contact your credit grantors at the first sign of any problems you might have in meeting your monthly obligations. In some cases your creditor will work with you in reducing the amount of your monthly payments. Additionally, you can seek the assistance of various non-profit consumer organizations such as the Consumer Credit Counseling Services, or the National Foundation for Credit Counseling.

Consumer Credit Counseling Services offer free or low-cost financial counseling to help people resolve their financial problems. CCCS can help you analyze your situation and work with you to develop solutions. You can reach them at 1-800-388-2227. In Atlanta, their web site is www.cccsatl.org. They also have a West Palm Beach, Florida, location (1-800-330-2227).

Eight Steps to Improving Your Credit

Getting out of debt has become more difficult since the introduction of the credit card. The buy-now-pay-later mind has put millions of consumers in position of fighting a difficult battle with debt. And overspending has no social boundaries. In fact, many families in financial trouble have two high incomes. To insure a good credit rating it is important to focus on paying your bills on time; however, as you acquire more debt you will find this becomes more difficult. If you find yourself falling behind:

1. Order copies of your credit report and score and analyze them carefully. By using the score simulator on the Equifax web site, you can see which factors most affect your credit score.

2. Establish a budget immediately to assess your spending habits.

3. Lock away your credit cards and don't use them; however, don't cancel them because if you have a low credit rating you may have trouble getting new cards. I heard one recommendation that I thought was funny at first, but upon further reflection it seems like a pretty good idea. Put your credit cards in a zip-lock bag and freeze them in a container of water in the back of your freezer. If you need them for an emergency, you still have them available. However, they are not available for impulse purchases.

4. Discuss ways with your family on how you can cut costs. Set goals and limits. This helps family members work together toward solutions that benefit everyone.

5. Use some of your savings to eliminate some portion of your debt, which may save you hundreds of dollars in interest.

6. Understand that applying for a new credit card may adversely affect your credit score.

7. Resolve to eliminate your debt. Either pay off the high-balance accounts, or pay off two or three smaller balances. Most experts will tell you to pay off your smallest outstanding balance first and eliminate that payment. Later, add that payment to your next smallest balance account and work your way up from there.

8. Avoid credit repair clinics that offer to remove late payments or bankruptcy.

Credit Repair Services

Don't confuse a legitimate credit counseling service, (i.e., one that belongs to a reputable membership organization that is independently accredited), with a "credit repair service." These unscrupulous credit repair services promise to end your credit woes with claims of "Easy credit to end all your money worries!" Others may claim to be able to remove an adverse credit record such as a judgment, lien or personal bankruptcy filing from your credit report. Such claims are false and misleading. In addition, any attempts by credit repair services to improve your credit history by modifying your identity could land you in trouble. According to the U.S. Federal Trade Commission you could be charged with wire or mail fraud if you use falsified credit data to apply for credit.

Beware of someone who wants to give you a new loan to get you out of debt. Borrowing to get out of debt is like overeating to lose weight. It doesn't work. Even if you consolidate your bills into one lower interest rate loan, there is a propensity to open up other credit lines and get right back in the same credit crunch.

Mortgage Lenders

What should you look for in a mortgage lender? I like to use a mortgage lender who has access to as many different lines or types of mortgages as possible. As I stated earlier, my current mortgage broker works for a small community bank. This gives me access to bank loans as well as Fannie Mae or Freddie Mac, or mortgage broker types of loans. It gives me access to more choices.

I also like to use a mortgage broker who owns rental properties. I would encourage you to contact your small community banks. You can contact your America Community Bankers Association (www.acbankers.org) in your state, and get their website where they will list the community banks in your area. In the state of Georgia it is the Community Bankers Association of Georgia. Their web site is www.cbaofga.com. You will type in your zip code and they will give you a list of the banks in your area. You may have to talk to as many as twenty mortgage brokers or bankers, but find somebody who has rental properties, has access to bank money, as well as traditional mortgage loans. You can also find mortgage lenders in the newspaper. Look in your Sunday paper for people who advertise for investment property loans and call them.

There are basically four types of mortgage loans:

1. Fixed rate loans.
2. Adjustable rate loans.
3. Convertible mortgage loans.
4. Balloon mortgage loans.

We will discuss each of these in detail.

Fixed rate loans.   Because they offer a monthly payment that is known and does not change, fixed rate mortgage loans remain the most popular type. Most fixed rate mortgages are for loan terms of 15 or 30 years. A 30-year loan offers lower payments but a slightly higher interest rate. For all of 2001 the average mortgage rate on a 30-year fixed rate loan was 6.97 percent, according to data from Freddie Mac. For 15 year mortgages the average rate was 6.5 percent. To pay off a fixed rate loan sooner, check with your lender to make sure you can make prepayments. You should be allowed to make these at any time and for any amount with no penalty. I like to get 30-year fixed rate mortgages, and then try to pay them off as soon as I can. That way I am obligated for the smaller amount.

Adjustable rate loans.   After an initial term the interest rate on an adjustable rate mortgage loan is reset periodically. This is to keep the rate in line with current market interest rates. For example a 3/1 ARM loan offers a fixed rate for the first three years, adjusting once a year thereafter. A 5/1 ARM loan offers a fixed rate for the first five years, adjusting yearly thereafter. The lender sets the interest rate by adding a margin to an index rate. Common indexes include:

- **Cost of fund index.** The eleventh district of Federal Home Loan Bank Board, which covers California, Nevada and Arizona, publishes the cost of fund index. For more information on the index, visit the website for the Federal Home Loan Bank of San Francisco, www.flhbsf.com.
- **Treasury bill yields.** The yield on a one-year T-bill adjusted for constant maturity security is widely used. Most loans

have a periodic rate cap and a lifetime cap to limit the amount the interest rate can increase each adjustment period, and over the term of the loan respectively. If you have a payment cap in your loan agreement you might face negative amortization of your loan. This has the effect of increasing the amount you owe.

Convertible mortgage loans. These are ARM loans that allow you to convert to a fixed rate loan after, at, or before a specified time. The conversion privilege lets you start off with a low variable rate, then lock in when fixed rates drop low enough.

Balloon mortgage loans. These are loans that often have interest only payments. In this case, you don't amortize any loan principle, and the entire loan amount is due at the end of the loan term. A balloon mortgage allows you to minimize your monthly payments until you re-finance the loan. Another advantage is that a larger share of your payment may be eligible for the interest tax deduction.

Meeting Your Lender

Once you call around and talk to several mortgage brokers, bankers or lenders, and find the type of product that you like, set an appointment to meet with them. When you go to meet with the mortgage lender bring all of this information with you:

- Two years complete tax returns.
- Two months of pay stubs.
- Three months of all of your bank statements.
- Three months of all of your brokerage account statements, including your Individual Retirement Accounts.
- Anything else your mortgage broker recommends.

The more information you can bring to the meeting, the more accurately they can give you a preapproval. A lender's preapproval is a commitment to fund your mortgage loan for a fixed period of time. A preapproval may include an interest rate lock preapproval, evaluates your credit history and calculates your housing and debt ratios. This is the ratio of how much you owe compared to how much you earn. You should expect to verify your income, length of employment and source of down payment. A preapproval legitimizes you as a serious buyer. It also gives you additional negotiating leverage to negotiate a sales price, especially if the seller cannot find other preapproved buyers. When seeking preapproval it is very important to not misrepresent the facts on your application. If a lender learns later that you misrepresented or omitted information on your application, your preapproval may be rescinded.

A preapproval may cost you a small amount of money for the lender to pull your credit report.

Bad Credit

What happens if you have bad credit? Does that disqualify you from the game? No, it does not. Even good people can fall on hard times, particularly with the current economy that includes layoffs, a stock market decline, and the dot bomb experiences. There you just have a little bit more work cut out for you. There have been careers made on people giving seminars and writing books on how to buy a house for someone who has bad credit, or no credit. I would also encourage you to order the Carlton Sheets program that you see advertised on the infomercials late at night, or by going to his website, www.carltonsheets.com. Other programs are available by John Adams at www.money99.com. You can also read some of Robert G. Allen's books. He wrote *No Money Down*. My favorite book on real estate that he wrote is *The Challenge*. My favorite of all Robert G. Allen books is *Multiple Streams of Income*, available at www.multiplestreamsofincome.com. For more information, log on to www.robertgallen.com. While we are listing web sites, sign up for my free newsletter at www.firstrentalhouse.com.

CHAPTER 3

Building a Winning Project Team

Whether you are looking at rental properties as a part-time venture or big-time business, one thing is for sure: You need a great team of professionals to help you succeed. Make sure you deal with people who have years of experience and a lot of knowledge in the area in which you are working. They can help you avoid making a lot of expensive mistakes. You cannot avoid making small mistakes, so concentrate on avoiding the BIG mistakes. For example, it may be worth paying more for a fifty-year-old attorney than to pay less for a thirty-year-old attorney, if the fifty-year-old attorney spent a lot of those years doing residential investment law. The opposite may also be true: The thirty-year-old may actually have more experience because he has five rental properties, and the fifty-year-old does not have any. I encourage you to find people who currently own rental properties. It will drastically change your relationship, as they will have empathy and special knowledge for your situation.

Who should be on your team? Here's your checklist:

- Mentors.
  - A banker or mortgage lender. If you have a friend or contact that is an appraiser, they could be a huge part of your team. Usually you do not get to pick your appraiser—the mortgage lender does that.
  - A real estate agent.
  - An attorney.
  - An accountant.
  - Contractors.

MENTORS

Most of my mentors are people I have yet to meet in person, but they have made a profound impact on my success, inspiring and educating me through their books, tapes, and seminars. These mentors include Carlton Sheets, Robert Kiyosaki, John Adams, and Dr. Wayne Dyer.

I live in a suburb of Atlanta. In case you have not heard, the traffic is legendary. It is not uncommon for families to move simply to reduce their commute. We did. We moved 15 miles closer to my office and condensed my commute by 45 minutes or longer depending on the weather. If you have a similar commute to your office, then this is a great opportunity to get into a good book. No, I do not want you reading a book in your car! Do not try that. Many books are available on tape. You can find many of them online at www.amazon.com.

Therefore, I listen to a large number of audiocassette tapes that I often get from the library. Even with audiocassettes available, I read a lot of books. I'm an auditory learner, meaning I learn better by listening than I do by reading. I was the kind of student in school who if I would just go to class and listen to the instructor every day, could get Bs and Cs in school. Therefore, listening to a lot of tapes while I am in the car works well for me. How about you? How do you spend your time in the car? This is a great way to benefit from those boring commutes!

Carlton Sheets is the gentleman you see on TV infomercials in the middle of the night talking about real estate. I have known several people over the years who say they have always been interested in rental real estate. I always suggest to these people that they get Carlton Sheets' program for $200. (See www.carltonsheets.com for testimonials and to view his product listings.) It is a really good background on how to get started and where to go. Carlton Sheets has a great program for the price he charges! The one complaint I've heard about his program is that he puts *too much* information in his kit and it overwhelms people. I bought his course many years ago and listened to it several times. (More on that in Chapter 4.) This program deals with the basics of buying a rental house. It covers where to find one and how to do the numbers to see if it is profitable. It does not deal as much with the mental side of why you want to invest in real estate, or why it is so hard to make that first step. Since I had a background in banking and mortgages, the numbers and calculations would come naturally to me. The psychology of making the first step made a more profound impact on me. That mental hurdle was reduced largely from Robert Kiyosaki. I would have considered this first deal successful if I had just broken even on money. The experience of the first deal would be the ultimate reward.

Robert Kiyosaki is author of the *New York Times* best-selling book *Rich Dad, Poor Dad*. He has also written several other books in his series that I have read. His book that really got me going on real estate is called *Retire Young, Retire Rich*. I highly recommend that book. It is a serious must read. If you really hate to read but would or could read just one book a year—this would be it. You have to read the whole book—the last 20 pages will get you going.

The point that really hit home with me was when Robert Kiyosaki stresses the fact that you are going to make mistakes, and that making mistakes is okay. The only way to accomplish anything is to make mistakes. People who do not make them do not accomplish anything because they take no risks. The key is to do your homework and reduce your risk with your investments. Once you understand that, and really get a grasp of that, you will not get mad at yourself as often when you do make mistakes. Get mad if you do not learn from them. They are the only way you can grow and develop when trying something new. Considering that I have never met the man, I think it is quite a statement to say he had a profound impact on me. That is why I include these mentors that I have never met. I encourage you to listen to people who have been there before you, and are the teachers of their craft. It is one skill to do it—it is a different skill to be able to explain it to people. When you find someone who can do both, get all you can get!

When I think of teaching my children how to swim, I remember the first time they let go of the side of the pool and took off to swim. It was not that they had any more skills than when they were hanging onto the side of the pool; it was just the fact that in their minds they believed they could do it. My mentors finally convinced me that I could do it. If they could do it, I could do it. They are certainly no smarter than I am, and I am no smarter than you are. At least I knew I had to believe that. If they could do it, I could do it, too. If I can do it, so can you. Hopefully, you will believe that faster than I did. I needed to hear that several times. My advice: Never give away or throw away a real estate investment book. Learn from my mistakes. My wife and I danced around the idea of buying a rental house for several years. During that time I would buy a book, then later give it to Goodwill or sell it at a garage sale. Then when we decided to go for it, the books were gone. It would have been nice to have had some of that information.

Robert Kiyosaki also has a board game called Cash Flow 101 where you actually play a board game of buying and selling businesses, rental houses, and apartment buildings. Playing the game taught me that this is a game! You know, buying this rental house, fixing it up, pulling the cash out, and getting the house rented—it is a game! This time on earth is a game, so get in it. This is not a practice round. Quit sitting on the sidelines. That was some of the motivation in my own personal life—to get off the sidelines and get into the game. Here I am with my first rental house, getting into the game, and scared to death! This is the unique perspective I offer my readers—the honest nervous feeling of the first time landlord. You can buy Kiyosaki's game at www.firstrentalhouse.com.

John Adams is a metro-Atlanta Carlton Sheets. In other words, he has his seminars, and he has his real estate books and an audio-cassette tape series in the metro-Atlanta area. He has been doing it for 20 years. He is a local man who is constantly giving seminars and selling audiocassette tapes and books on how to do rental houses in the metro-Atlanta area. He was very encouraging, and he has a $100 program that I bought called *The Landlord's Survival Guide*. It also came with an audiocassette tape called *The Top Ten Mistakes That Landlords Make*. That audiocassette tape is worth $1,000 in my opinion! I urge you to go to his web site, www.money99.com, and look under the books and tapes sections to get the landlording program. That audiocassette tape is a college education in itself. Although John's program is targeted to Georgia, 90 percent of the information will be valuable to you no matter where you live. The survival guide covers information about how to present yourself to the renter, how to market the house, even hints on things to include in your lease. John also has a radio program that should be available over the Internet.

Dr. Wayne Dyer is a psychologist who has a large number of books and audiocassette tapes on self-manifestation, realizing your dreams, and finding your destiny. I listened to a six-tape audiocassette tape series called *Transformation: You'll See It When You Believe It*. Dyer's product info puts it this way:

> Thought is everything! These three words can change your life forever. You already have everything needed for a thoroughly happy life. Dr. Dyer simply shows you how to make use of those innate abilities to

make almost anything happen. You'll learn his technique for finding abundance in your life—by visualizing that you already have what you want, you'll get it!

His books and audiocassettes are available at www.nightingale-conant.com. He really talks about picturing in your mind the exact outcome that you want. You may have already learned that many successful people do this. Many golfers will picture the shot in their mind before they actually hit the ball. A number of professional athletes picture their performance in their mind before they perform it. I constantly had in my mind that I was going to buy a rental house, possibly a foreclosure, fix it up, pull the cash out, and find a tenant with a positive cash flow. Picture yourself picking up that first rent check!

Robert G. Allen wrote some of the most popular real estate books including *Nothing Down* and *The Challenge*. I also listened to Robert G. Allen's *Multiple Streams of Income*. Among the 18 chapters are 3 ways to make money on real estate.

1. Rental houses.
2. Foreclosures and "flippers".
3. Paying other people's taxes.

It was great reinforcement for what I had been reading from other authors. He writes in detail about nine ways to find super real estate bargains and the five most powerful nothing-down techniques. Chapter 9 goes through the foreclosure process and all the different times you can purchase the property. The house I bought was a foreclosed house—the bank owned it. I did not set out looking just for foreclosures. However, the number of foreclosed houses was at an all-time high. Therefore, I had a good supply to choose from. There are 100 ways to make money in real estate—you just need to pick one to get started. *Just get started.*

These are the mentors whom I never met. You can have the very same mentors, and others, without ever having to meet them. Looking through the tapes that I have in my car today, I see that I borrowed many of them from the library. Talk about cheap mentors!

Now, let us talk about the team members whom I know personally and work with on a regular basis! I will also continue to work with these people in the future.

THE BANKER OR MORTGAGE LENDER

One of the instrumental people on my team, as I went through this rental house project, was my loan broker, Jill. She works at The Community Bank in Loganville, Georgia (770-466-6482 or e-mail jillc@gotcb.com), where she has access to the bank's internal lending capabilities, as well as brokering outside the bank with major wholesalers. Some of your community banks have terms and types of loans that the traditional mortgage broker will not have.

If you want to try rental housing, I encourage you to develop relationships with some small town community bank lenders. You can find these people by looking in your yellow pages for your state's Community Bankers Association. In the state of Georgia it is called Community Bankers Association of Georgia. They have a list (www.cbaofga.com) of the community banks in your area. For outside Georgia, go to your favorite search engine, like www.google.com or www.ask.com, and look for Community Banks (your state), and you should be directed to your state's web site. Or just simply call the community banks in your local area and talk to the mortgage broker. From there you can ask what kind of loan programs they have available for buying houses out of foreclosure, or renovating a house, and so on. They will be able to walk you through the details. You may find that the smaller banks may treat you differently from the big banks—your personality and business background may dictate whom you use. Generally community banks have more flexibility, and the decision makers are all local.

My twenty-eight-year-old nephew said he learned more by talking to a loan broker and a real estate agent for 20 minutes each than he did by reading some of the books on the subject. That might be a key step for you. If you have more questions than 20 minutes will cover, offer to take them to breakfast or lunch. I like breakfast—people are not as hurried and appreciate the change. Of course you do not want to hit them with a barrage of questions, but give them an opportunity to give you advice. People love to dish out advice. Be a sponge and take it all in. It will also help you develop a relationship. Be sure to explain up front that this interview is only informational.

Your mortgage broker at the bank is going to be able to give you your preapproval. They may also have access and contacts with some of the better realtors in your local area who will be able to help you with the type of houses you might be looking for. In dealing with your mortgage broker, try to find one who already owns some rental property. You want to have a mortgage broker who understands exactly what you are going through. They may be able to help you with tenant issues or guide you toward attorneys or CPAs and so on. You will be surprised at the contacts your community banker has.

THE REAL ESTATE AGENT

My real estate agent, Tommy Blackwell of Remax (770-209-0595 or on the Web at www.tommyblackwell.com), has been a friend for the past six or seven years whom I got to know from church. He moved to a different part of town and switched churches. But we kept in contact once or twice a year, just seeing what each other was doing. He formerly sold commercial real estate, and the winter before my first rental purchase he switched over to residential. He sent out a standard letter that is routinely sent out when someone gets into residential real estate. The purpose of the letter was to say to family and friends "Here is my card. If you know of anyone looking for a house, let me know." I got the letter and the card, and I called Tommy and told him what we were looking for. We got him the preapproval letter, so he knew we were serious. He works for Remax, and one of the agents in his franchise had a number of listings of foreclosed houses from a particular bank. That is a big benefit of working with a large organization—he had someone in his office who had a key contact. This may not be available if you work with a small office that has only two or three brokers. However, there is a very small real estate company in a small town nearby that appears to get many foreclosures, and lower prices on housing. The moral of this story is—do your homework.

Foreclosures work a bit differently for real estate agents from a single residential listing. Because of this, not all agents will take a foreclosure—they are time consuming during the listing phase. The agents who do tend to take a large number of them. Often, they get all the listings from one institutional lender. You need to locate an office with one of these foreclosure specialists. Why? You want to be the first to know. Once the agent lists a house, it may take a couple of days before the house hits the multiple listing services. Therefore, you want to know about it before everyone else in town. If your agent is in the same office, they will have access to this information.

When this particular house that we bought came on the market, Tommy called me and said that the man who handles these things just put this one on the market. He said we needed to look at it *that day* as it would sell quickly. We would need to make an offer quickly. He said it would take $5,000 to $10,000 in work. If I wanted in the game, this was a textbook case of a renovation house. I told him that if he thought it was worth looking at, I trusted his judgment and I would meet him at the house today. Tommy was instrumental in walking me through this house and showing me that it was not in as bad shape as I initially had thought. He repeatedly pointed out that it was really in need of a lot of cosmetics: paint, steam clean the carpet, clean up the bathrooms, clean the floors, pressure wash the house—simple types of repairs. Otherwise, the house was structurally sound. The water heater, furnace, and air conditioner were in great shape. He was able to help me see the final product, and that it was not as bad as it had first looked to me.

The first time I looked at the house, I said, "Tommy, there is no way. This place is disgusting, and this is way over my head." He said, "Doug, stop and look around. The walls need paint, the carpets need steam cleaning." He was right. There were no holes in the carpets, and the walls just needed paint. We ended up doing a lot more work than that, but you would expect a salesperson like Tommy to do a job like that. He was excellent at going through all the details of the house. He also suggested we not overdo the renovation, which, by the way, is a pitfall to watch for. Just because I do not like the kitchen cabinets does not mean the house will not rent. (We painted the cabinets white!)

When you are looking for a realtor, there are several places where you can go to find one.

- Ask your friends for referrals. For example, if you belong to a large church, ask some of the senior members of the church who the realtors are, and go have breakfast or lunch with them. Tell them your requirement and ask them whom they recommend. Again, people love to give advice. You can get a lot of information for a $7.00 meal.
- Go to the web site of a particular local franchise; some of them have the ability to pick on a specialty to find an agent. For example, at the Remax site you can pick specialties, and you can find people in your zip code or area who specialize in investment properties. That will save you a lot of time and get you to the proper people. Once you see an agent you think might work for you, call them for an informational meeting.
- Find agents who also have rental properties, or have other clients who have rental properties. They will be able to answer questions that you will have.

You may have to talk to five or six real estate agents to find the right one. But do not get discouraged. I met another real estate agent at a seminar. The seminar on government grants and subsidies turned out to be disappointing. But one of the activities that the seminar speaker had us do was shake hands with all the people around us. A woman in front of me put her hand up over her shoulder to shake my hand, told me her name, and said she was a realtor. During the seminar I passed her a note that said "I buy real estate, 80 percent of appraised value. I can close in 7 to 10 days," and I also told her the parts of town that I was interested in. I designated three to four bedrooms. I gave her my telephone numbers and my e-mail address, and also told her that I had a preapproval letter. At this point she knew I was serious; I was giving her all the different ways to contact me and the type of house I wanted to buy. She immediately handed me a business card. At the end of the seminar, she turned around and said to me, "I have a house that is not even on the market yet. Would you like to go look at it?" You just never know where your next real estate agent, or your next contact, is going to come from. Keep an open mind.

We did look at the house and one that was listed two doors down. You will learn why we did not buy that house later in the book, but even though I did not buy that house, I am still on her radar screen. Next time she gets a fixer upper, I hope she will think of me!

ATTORNEYS

Typically, you will deal with an attorney only for the closing of your mortgage. This relationship is not nearly as personal as you will want your mortgage broker and real estate agent to be. However, you do want to feel comfortable with their level of knowledge and competence.

If you work with a real estate agent, they will have an attorney in their office they prefer to work with. I have not found this to be a problem. They will be very good at real estate closings or they will not continue to get their business. My mortgage broker (Jill) has an attorney whom she prefers to deal with—and guess what—he owns two rental houses. I have not had a problem with him, either. Sometimes it is nice to work with a team because if there are any problems, they already have a relationship, and do not get mad at each other or point fingers.

If your real estate agent, or your mortgage broker, really has a preferred closing attorney, I would start out there until something goes wrong. You can obviously call and talk to them, but this is not something that you want to argue over. It is worth an extra $50 in closing costs, if they are going to get it right and record your title properly. Do not be afraid to pay for good help.

I also found a closing attorney when I was a member of a Lead-Sharing Club. These groups gather usually on a weekly basis to share business leads. In Atlanta one such company is called Powercore (details at www.powercore.net). They have about 30 clubs around metro-Atlanta. Other lead sharing companies that I have heard of are Freedom Builders and La Tip. I met my co-author Sean Lyden at a Powercore meeting. It works similar to a Chamber of Commerce meeting in that you get to network your contacts with each other. In Powercore, we had one mortgage broker, one real estate agent, one pest control guy, one mechanic, and so on. We all shared leads in the club. One of the members of the club was a closing attorney. He and I have become friends. And now he has a rental house, and if I ever need someone else to review a contract, or help me with one, I can call on Ben to help me do that.

Again, there are a variety of places and ways to find your attorneys. If you are a member of a large church, ask your senior parishioners who is a good closing attorney for real estate. You want to be certain to use a real estate attorney, not a divorce attorney, not a litigation attorney. You want to use someone who specializes in real estate.

ACCOUNTANTS

Usually, your real estate attorneys are going to know the better accountants in that area. Also, if your mortgage banker has several rental properties, find out who his or her CPA or accountant is. Your real estate agent will also have contacts. Use people who have years of experience in the business; they will know which professionals have the better expertise in that area. My accountant specializes in working with small business owners, real estate professionals, and also owns two rental houses. He also set me up with an attorney who helped with my corporation paperwork. I have an LLC corporation for my company for liability reasons. Therefore, it was necessary that the attorney and the CPA work as a team. That will help to reduce finger pointing of filing the corporations and getting my taxes paid properly.

CONTRACTORS

A big part of my team consists of the contractors. This is where I spent the majority of my time pulling my hair out—or what is left of it. All the previous mentors, and parts of my team, were much easier to deal with than the contractors, especially the ones I never met! I wanted to do a large portion of the work myself, but I still needed some contractors to do some specialized work. This took a lot of telephone time and patience in dealing with different people. Here is what to expect when you call a contractor:

1. He comes out at his scheduled time and he is on time.
2. He gives a quote detailing all procedures.
3. The quote is fair—you let him know he has the job.
4. He starts work two days later. He finishes in one day and gets it all done right the first time.
5. He is under budget.
6. *You* need to wake up because you are Oh *Soooo Dreaming*!!

Maybe we should all forget real estate and become electricians and plumbers. I will go into details about personal experiences with contractors in Chapter 10. However, I never had any problems with my plumber or electrician. It helps to know him socially and pay him *immediately*.

One way I found a great contractor was from the Lead-Sharing Club that I mentioned earlier. Through those contacts I met a man by the name of Skip Johnson (owns six rental houses), who has a business called Top to Bottom Services (770-967-2255), and he has multiple skills as he fixes electrical, plumbing, and other problems. He fixes things from the top to the bottom of the house. He does not fix appliances or gas lines, but everything else in the house. When we moved from one house to another last November, we had him install a bathroom in the basement and build a laundry room on the second floor of the house. It was necessary for him to run electrical and plumbing lines. He also tore down part of a wall and built in a couple of other walls.

I like someone who can do both electrical and plumbing, so you can make one phone call and get several things accomplished. I encourage finding someone with these skills, because with one phone call you can get both plumbing and electrical and some carpentry work done, and avoid having travel time billed by separate contractors.

You can also simplify your scheduling. Some renovation projects may work like this:

1. You need a plumber to first run the plumbing lines.
2. Then an electrician runs the wiring.
3. The sheet rock is hung, finished, and painted.
4. The plumber has to come back to install the faucets/toilets, and so on.
5. The electrician has to come back to install the outlets, light fixtures, and so on. I think you can see the hassle and time delays in getting all this scheduled and completed.

I have seen advertised flyers in my mailbox for handyman type of services for people who are licensed in both plumbing and electrical. This seems to be a growing trend in contractors. Contact two or three, or more, interview them, and get some of their referrals. Deal with the people who show up on time to give you an estimate and whom you feel most comfortable with in your house. Check to make sure they have insurance in case they cause more damage than they fix. Word of caution—call their insurance agent and verify their insurance. They should not mind if you ask for proof of insurance. One of my contractors is a tree service. In my rental house, they were called right away to remove a dead tree. When they give a quote for a job, they always enclose a copy of their liability policy complete with agent name and phone number. If a contractor does not have insurance, anything they damage could be your responsibility. For example, Trent the Tree Cutter (fictitious name) gives you this unbelievable deal to remove that dead limb hanging over the kitchen. Trent picks a windy, rainy day to remove the limb. He climbs out over the roof, and *snap*—Trent and the tree limb are now in your attic! The rain is now dripping on the hardwood floors in the kitchen. Do you think Trent should pay for the thousands of dollars worth of damage? Of course you do. Did you drift back into that dream again?

One of the keys to getting repeat service from contractors, especially mom-and-pop contractors, is to pay them immediately upon invoice, because the next time you call them, they will remember you were the customer who paid his bill on time. They are going to be far more inclined to come do your work than the guy who takes 45 to 60 days to pay his bills. Whenever I deal with a small organization, or a one- or two-man contractor crew, I always pay those people immediately upon invoice. It is amazing how well you get treated the next time. Put yourself in their shoes. You, the painter, have a customer, Joe, who pays on time and will need you again on another house. Joe calls during a busy time. How inclined will you be to work on Joe's job? I certainly would be. Be the customer you would want to have!

The most difficult contractor I had to deal with was the glass repairman. I had a broken window on the front of the house, and it literally took one month to repair because they had to order that glass three different times to get the right size to repair the window. The repair proved frustrating. I also had a sliding glass door that needed glass replaced because the seal was broken. The door worked fine; however, moisture had gotten in between the two panes of glass and you could not see outside. They did a great job with the sliding glass door. It worked well and was done on time. The window was a pane! (Just a little rental house humor!)

I have had good luck with contractors, and I have had bad luck with contractors. My carpet cleaning man cussed me out. He had booked my job incorrectly. I was on his schedule for the wrong day. I was venting frustration when, all of a sudden, he didn't know how to handle an upset client. He cussed at me and hung up the phone. I could not believe it. I called the company back and told them what the dispatcher had done. He called me back, apologized, and tried to get back my business. It was too late. I had already gotten out the yellow pages and called the largest ad. The new contractor was there that afternoon and did a great job. It was probably all for the best that I did not use the first company for the job. Just understand, you are going to get all kinds of experiences when you become a landlord, from the good, to the bad, to the ugly.

My subdivision newsletter also had a referral list of contractors. This is another good way to find contractors in your area to get referrals. You might talk to your next-door neighbors about whom they have used and who did good work. As you know, home ownership alone gives you the opportunity to have a referral list!

For more information on building your winning real estate team, consult these resources:

- *Becoming a Landlord by Fannie Mae*. Available through the Consumer Resource Center, 800-732-6643. Ask about training classes available in selected cities, www.fanniemae.com.

- *Every Landlord's Legal Guide* by Nolo Press, www.nolo.com, 800-992-6656.
- American Association of Small Property Owners, www. aaspo.org, 202-625-8330.
- National Real Estate Investors Association, www.national reia.com, 888-762-7342.

You can log on to my web site at www.firstrentalhouse.com to see before and after pictures of my rental house renovations, book signing dates, and my free newsletter.

MOTIVATIONAL QUOTE

The future belongs to those who believe in the beauty of their dreams.

Eleanor Roosevelt

CHAPTER 4

Getting over the Hump!

Please do not think that I just woke up one day and thought "Hey, I'm gonna buy a rental house today!" And then two or three weeks later I made an offer and bought my first rental house. It just was not that easy.

The reality is that I had been considering doing rental houses for several years. In fact, about 10 years ago I looked at a quadruplex that already had four renters. I ran the numbers and they, unfortunately, seemed to make sense. Since I did not have the cash for the down payment, my strategy on that deal was to leverage or use the equity in my permanent residence for the down payment. My other financial obligations at that time included a $300 per month car payment. I was going to use the equity line of credit to pull some cash out for the down payment on the investment property and pay off my car. If everything worked out according to plan on the quadruplex, I would net $400 a month in positive cash flow. In other words, I would have gone from a negative $300 a month for the car payment to a positive $400 a month positive cash flow, translating into a $700 per month upward swing in my personal income. A no-brainer, right? Well, I didn't do the deal. I was scared. All it took was my wife saying, "Do you really want to be a landlord?" That was enough to nix the deal!

There was something about getting into a quadruplex and managing four renters I had not qualified or chosen that seemed too overwhelming for me to take on. At the time, we were not sure that we wanted to be landlords, especially taking on such a big project. Also, upon closer analysis of just the outside, the quadruplex unit itself had some deferred maintenance (diplomatic for "it looked like a dump")—cracked paint, rotting window frames, rotting decks, and so on. It was also quite a distance from my home, with a commute time of 30 to 45 minutes. I was not very familiar with that area, although the unit was in an appreciating part of town. While Nan and I went back and forth over the decision for almost a month, we decided to pass. In hindsight, it would have put us "in the game" so much earlier and we could have already amassed a portfolio of rentals by now. However, it would have been an education multiplied by four. Soon after that deal Nan got pregnant with our first child and we had no time for looking at rental properties. Looking back—I should have done that deal—traffic along that corridor is getting heavier every year and it is pretty close to town so it is attractive just for its location. I drove through that neighborhood last week and found the quadruplex I looked at almost 10 years ago. It was like looking at lost treasure. The neighborhood looks a little run down—but then you will get that feeling in an apartment complex full of quadruplexes. I like the atmosphere of single-family houses better. Even though I now think I should have done that deal, it is also probably better to start with only one renter. Someday I may own a multiunit high rise—but not for my first deal.

Getting over the Hump!

In 1994 there were 11 duplexes for sale in Buford, Georgia, about 15 minutes from my home. They were in a subdivision of duplexes, with about 30 units total. The developer still owned 11 duplexes. I tried to structure a deal to buy all 11 of them, with no money down. Since I knew the developer probably had little of his money invested in the duplexes, I proposed an owner financing deal. The offer was about $1,100,000 (one of Donald Trump's suggestions is to think big!). At the time, I was thirty-two with no landlord experience. That pretty much sums up why the deal did not work out! A month later I ended up putting an offer in on one of the duplexes pending the final inspection. Both sides of the duplex were currently rented. The offer was accepted, but when we had the inspection done on the house, it had multiple code violations and structural problems.

- There were water drainage problems that had caused the entry doorways to rot. There seemed no easy way to solve this issue.
- The siding had been installed poorly and some of the structural wood was rotting. Although this could have been repaired, it made me question the quality of the rest of the construction.
- There was evidence of previous fire damage. The inspector discovered this by crawling around in the attic and then got the full story by interviewing one of the tenants. It was possible for fire damage to not do permanent damage; however, I did not want to take the chance.
- The furnace was located in a closet off the kitchen. The bifold doors had been installed too close to the furnace, causing a potential fire hazard.

The $300 inspection saved us untold heartache (and money!) because it would have been very difficult to sell that house one day down the road. There were serious problems with it.

About six years ago we were considering putting in an offer on a triplex about a mile and a half from our house. The entire subdivision was in a rental area and had about eight quadruplexes and three triplexes that were all for sale. I put in an offer on one of the triplexes that I knew I could afford. At the time we still were not sure that we wanted to be landlords. And, as before, we would take on three tenants that we had not screened and did not know. The property already had a manager who was going to continue to manage the property. That deal ended up with all the buildings going to one buyer. Again, you can understand why the seller preferred to sell to one guy.

We have wrestled constantly with this idea of buying rental properties. While we looked at several different rental properties over the years, we just never had the self-confidence to pull the trigger and move forward until recently. Here is how we got over the hump.

Take Action Despite Your Fears

You feel mixed emotions as you consider spending your hard earned money on your real estate business. One moment you are so pumped you cannot think about anything else. But the next, you are stricken with fear, intimidated by the uncertainty that lies ahead. ("What if I fail and go broke? What do I even know about starting a business, anyway? What would I do if the water heater broke in the middle of the night?") Intimidation is a feeling that somehow you are not good enough to succeed. You do not always see your potential, but rather your limitations. You feel doubt and uncertainty about whether you are up to the challenges that the real estate business throws your way.

Every aspiring real estate investor gets intimidated to some degree. That is a given. How do you overcome those feelings of intimidation to fulfill your dream?

Learn, Learn, Learn . . .

The more you know about the real estate business, the less intimidated you will be when you are confronted with new situations. The book that really pushed me over the edge was Robert Kiyosaki's book *Retire Young, Retire Rich*. That book gave me the self-confidence to get me off the fence and go forward. Kiyosaki stresses that you spend your time and money on assets that go up in value and create residual income. The rental house business plan is to have the house go up in value, creating long-term wealth, while it creates residual income and tax benefits today. It is the combination of the house appreciation, the depreciation on taxes, the tax breaks, and the deposit of cash flow that make it the grand slam of creating wealth.

How do you get over the learning curve? Block out 10 to 30 minutes each day to read publications and books. (See appendix for recommended publications and books to help you succeed in your real estate business.) Listen to tapes while you are in your car. I listen to them over and over until I get to the point where I think, "Hey, I *can* do this stuff! There's no reason why I shouldn't succeed at this!" Attend seminars. Learn more about the tax benefits (which are huge and unfortunately constantly changing), the cash flow benefits, and strategies for creating substantial, long-term wealth. The more knowledge you gain, the more confident you will be to move forward toward your investment goals.

Do Not Fear Failure

Even some of the most celebrated real estate moguls, like Donald Trump, have (at times) fallen on hard times with their investments. Yet even with failure comes a learning curve that can help you be successful in your next project.

For example, perhaps what is holding you back is the fear you will not find tenants for your new rental house. You start agonizing "What will I do? What happens if I lose my shirt over this?" To overcome this fear, put things in their proper perspective. Do not look at any single episode as defeat but as a way of finding out what you have to do better. Tom Hopkins, in his book, *How to Master the Art of Selling*, suggests repeating the following five affirmations, which he calls 5 Attitudes Toward Rejection.

1. I never see failure as failure, but only as a learning experience.
2. I never see failure as failure, but only as the negative feedback I need (in order) to change course in my direction.
3. I never see failure as failure, but only as the opportunity to develop my sense of humor.
4. I never see failure as failure, but only as the opportunity to practice my techniques and perfect my performance.
5. I never see failure as failure, but only as the game I must play to win.

Count the Cost of Fear

You want to call the shots, earn unlimited income, and set your own schedule, right? Then you cannot afford to allow fear to stop you from pursuing your real estate business! This is exactly what Nan and I had to come to terms with. When I found myself terrified of taking the first steps, I would ask myself "Am I willing to give up my dream for this fear?" The answer to this question was all I would need to get me moving toward our goals. Again, make a list of your fears and research them. What you may be afraid of is what you do not know. Learning more about the subject of your fear will start the process of eliminating it.

Create Your Own Daily Challenge

Identify the activity that intimidates you the most, and make that your top priority for the day. Then do it! It is kind of like riding a bike for the first time. You are scared to death of falling—then you fall, but you get up thinking "Man, that was not so bad!" From that point on, you are a daredevil. Take the same approach with your real estate business. When you confront intimidating situations head-on, you will find yourself feeling more and more confident. For example, if you are afraid of doing any rehab, start small at your current residence. You know that bedroom you use as an office? Wouldn't you love to have it repainted?

Now that you have a project, you need a plan. First, you want to start with the paint. After deciding the color that best fits your room, visit your local home improvement warehouse for an education on paint. I recommend you make that visit during the week. The do-it-yourself customers flood the place on weekends. Therefore, if you go on a Tuesday, you will be there with the contractors, who do not ask the staff for help. I have had great success with this approach. Simply tell them you have never painted a wall in your life. They will walk you around explaining the difference between a flat finish and an eggshell finish. They will show you the tools to use and the right way to clean up the mess when you are done. Most home improvement stores give classes on Saturdays on a variety of projects. Nan, who has a bachelor of science degree in chemistry and no construction training, took the ceramic tile class one Saturday morning. She has since tiled four bathrooms and a laundry room. She was able to do this because she watched home improvement shows on television and attended a free class. Another advantage in her tiling endeavor was she started small. Therefore, if it did not look good, it was not much to repair. The location was also not critical. She started with the bathroom in the basement. So when you choose that first painting project do not make it the second story foyer that everyone will notice and critique! Start out painting the inside of your garage.

Cannot think of a project to do around your place, or are afraid of what you might do on your own? Okay, volunteer to help someone else. You can try a friend, (a really good friend!) or better yet you and a friend can donate your time to a project like Habitat for Humanity. They provide low-cost housing to families who could not afford a house otherwise. A Habitat for Humanity recipient is required to work a minimum number of hours for the organization. They depend heavily on volunteers to complete the projects. They have new construction and renovating projects, and you can gain an education and be of service at the same time. There are other organizations that also do the same thing. Since Habitat for Humanity was started in Georgia, and former President Jimmy Carter and his wife Rosalyn are active in the program, it is the best known in our area.

Find Successful Mentors to Strengthen Your Resolve

As we talked about before, mentors are excellent resources to motivate you in your real estate endeavors. I have several friends who own rental houses. A couple in particular, Drue and Elaine, were trying to sell their home and move to a better neighborhood. They could not get the price for their house that they wanted, so they decided to pull out the equity with an equity line of credit for the down payment on their next house. Then they rented out their current home.

Here's how it worked out for Drue and Elaine. They had a mortgage payment of approximately $1,000 per month. They took out an equity line of credit of $20,000 to acquire their new home, costing them $250 per month. Therefore, their total monthly outflow on their first home was $1,250. But they rented it for $1,350 per month, giving them a $100 positive monthly cash flow. In other words, they were able to acquire a new house, and at the same time, turned their current house into a revenue generator.

The rental house thing seemed to work well for them and gave me the feeling that if they could do it, so could I! This is one instance, among others, that increased my self-confidence to go forward and try buying my own rental house. Find a friend who is just as nervous as you are and make a bet with them. First one to buy a house and get it rented gets $50. That may be the motivation you need to get yourself to make the following needed two turns:

1. *Turn* off the TV. Make a chart and track how much time you spend watching television. You be the judge! Are you wast-

ing valuable learning time? Do not get me wrong. I watch a lot of television, but I also read a lot. Television can be a great learning tool. Nan and I enjoy home improvement shows. We have both learned a lot about construction and renovation. Unfortunately, when she sees something on TV, she wants to try it at home. She has a fascination for tearing down walls!

2. *Turn* the lock on the door handle behind you. Get out of your house and look at some property. It is relatively painless. You will get an education on home values for the cost of a few gallons of gasoline. You may just stay so busy, you will forget what it was you were afraid of!

How do you find a mentor who is right for you—and can help you get over the hump in buying your first rental house?

Begin your search by thinking about highly successful people you know. They could be your friends, relatives, your friends' relatives, or people you have met at networking functions whom you admire and want to emulate.

Next, know what you expect from a mentor. Look for someone with these qualities:

- Has your best interests in mind. Your mentor should want to see you succeed nearly as much as you do.
- Is someone with whom you feel comfortable sharing sensitive personal and business information. For your mentor to truly understand your situation, he may need to know:

    Approximately how much money you have in a savings account.

    A general range of your income.

    Your debt service. That means how much debt you have, and what your monthly payments are.

Not all mentors will need to know this information. However, you should be prepared to share your personal finances.

- Offers objective advice. Look for someone who will actually tell you the truth. Many of us hate to hurt someone's feelings. However, you need accurate advice, not *nice* advice.
- Understands you. In addition to knowing how to make money in real estate or how to enter the business, your mentor has to understand your abilities. If this is someone who does not know you personally, tell him or her about yourself. By this time you should know what your strengths and weaknesses are. Your mentor can help you work through areas that need improvement.

Where do you meet potential mentors? Start attending networking functions sponsored by the following organizations:

- Local real estate investment clubs. Ask your real estate agent, your mortgage broker, and your mentor.
- Local chambers of commerce. You can find the phone number in your local phone book, or through the Internet.
- Civic organizations like Optimist International, Rotary, or Kiwanis—these will be listed in the phone book or on the Internet.
- Business referral networking groups. Professions often in lead sharing groups could be real estate agents, chiropractors, mortgage brokers, and insurance agents. These are generally people who deal with the public.
- Ask your banker if they have any customers who might be interested. Think about how flattered you would be if your banker asked if you would mentor a customer. Some people have a large ego that needs to be fed! If the customer is indeed flattered, the banker has scored a few brownie points.

Get to know successful people in real estate. How did they do it? What mistakes did they make and how did they overcome their errors? By spending time with mentors, you gain the knowledge, inspiration, and motivation you need to move forward and succeed with your first rental house.

Use Affirmations

Remember Stuart Smalley? You know, the guy on *Saturday Night Live* who would gaze into the mirror and, with a plastered smile, recite aloud, "I'm good enough. I'm smart enough. And, doggone it, people *like* me." Do not let this spoof put a bad taste in your mouth about using affirmations: They can actually make the difference in giving you the courage you need to buy your first rental house. The key is to use affirmations properly.

How do you create affirmations that work for you? Ron Guzik is a motivational speaker and business consultant in Glendale Heights, Illinois. In his book *The Inner Game of Entrepreneuring*, he shows readers how to achieve the various psychological qualities entrepreneurs need to succeed. The following are four tips:

1. *Make affirmations personal.* The purpose of using affirmations, according to Guzik, is to reinforce a personal trait that you want to see developed or changed in your life. For example, if you are a chronic procrastinator, repeat to yourself something like "I am on top of things, and I follow up on projects with energy and attention to detail." Try something pertinent to real estate investment. " I am an excellent landlord. I can select the right property at the right price, and choose the right tenants."

2. *Use the present tense.* "Many of the people who do brain research today believe your day-to-day actions come out of your subconscious mind," says Guzik. "Positive, present-tense affirmations are about trying to encourage,

reinforce and build the subconscious beliefs you want to have in the future."

3. *Be specific.* Guzik likens using affirmations to setting goals. "You don't want generic or vague goals," says Guzik. "You want a specific target you're aiming for; then you focus your consciousness and attention on that target. It's the same thing with your affirmations." You may want to focus on buying that *first* rental house.

4. *Invoke feeling.* "Many times when people have goals, what they really want are the feelings they get when they achieve their goal: the feelings of pride, satisfaction and accomplishment," Guzik observes. "When you use affirmations, try to bring those (feelings) into the process." That is the feeling that drives many of us to financial freedom. Think positively about real estate giving us financial freedom.

When should you use affirmations? The most critical time is when negative thoughts start to creep into your mind. "Often the things we say to ourselves are not encouraging, not supportive, and there's a lot of feedback from the outside world that, generally speaking, is not positive," Guzik notes. "Affirmations are a way of counteracting (negative self-talk) with positive things you're moving toward—things you're trying to achieve." Guzik also suggests planning time in your day to recite affirmations, preferably three times a day: morning, afternoon, and evening. This way, you stay focused on what you want to achieve throughout the day.

Stuart Smalley aside, Guzik admits he always repeats his affirmations in front of a mirror. Whether you choose to say your affirmations in the shower or in the car as you commute to and from the office, the main thing is that you do it on a consistent basis. To that end, Guzik advises, "Choose a routine that works with your life."

ACTION STEP

Log on to www.firstrentalhouse.com and order Cash Flow 101 from Robert Kiyosaki. This game will let you practice the business of buying and selling houses and businesses before spending any major capital. The game will cost you a couple of hundred dollars but may save you thousands of dollars in mistakes. It gave me the courage to take the next step. That is what your first rental house is all about.

MOTIVATIONAL QUOTES

Accept the challenges, so that you may feel the exhilaration of victory.
General George S. Patton

Progress always involves risk; you can't steal second base and keep your foot on first.
Frederick Wilcox

CHAPTER 5

Getting the Government to Pay Your Rent!

When I talk to people about buying rental houses, what holds many of them back is the fear of being a landlord—in other words, the fear they will have to be the bad guy in getting tenants to pay rent on time. Well, if you want a piece of the real estate pie but do not want a lot of the rent collection hassles, the U.S. government has the answer for you! Take advantage of Section 8 housing and let the government make most of the rent payments for you. They will even direct deposit the money!

Think about the advantages of Section 8 housing:

- You receive guaranteed housing assistance payments on a monthly basis deposited in your account on the first business day of each month.
- The Department of Community Affairs staff will assist you with all required paperwork.

■ Your monthly contract rent amount will not be affected regardless of any changes in family income.

What is in it for the federal government? Well, politicians have long been looking for an answer to providing low-income housing to those who need it. The challenge, however, has been that government sponsored housing projects would quickly deteriorate and become hotbeds for crime and drug use. And since the tenants typically did not have much accountability in maintaining the properties themselves, these housing projects would cost a lot of government money for maintenance and repairs. Remember the high-rise, multistory housing projects of the 1970s and 1980s? Chances are good they are no longer standing. That is because the plan was not working.

Then along came the Department of Housing and Urban Development (HUD) with a groundbreaking idea: Why not partner with the private sector to provide low-income housing at a much lower cost of management and maintenance? In fact, rather than the federal government being the landlord, let us pay John Q. Public to be the landlord! After all, private landlords would have a vested interest in managing and maintaining the property because . . . well . . . they would *own* the property!

Hence, you have Section 8, the government's way to partner with you, in the private sector, to provide safe, affordable housing for disabled and low-income people.

HOW DOES SECTION 8 WORK?

Here is how it works. HUD issues a housing voucher based on several factors, including the number of people in the family, age of the children, and number of bedrooms needed. So, for example, if you advertise a three-bedroom house and your prospective Section 8 tenants have a two-bedroom voucher, you're not going to get much money. The Section 8 payment you receive is based on the number of bedrooms and current comparable rent for that number of bedrooms in that area. And note that there is a cap on how much Section 8 will pay. So do not think your $250,000 subdivision home is going into the Section 8 housing pool with positive cash flow! The actual rent cap varies per county.

For example, in 2003 HUD approved $1,150 per month for a three-bedroom house in Gwinnett County. A three-bedroom house in a more rural area of Georgia could have a limit of $900 per month. However, this does not mean you will get the maximum listed. Your Section 8 office will set a rental limit for your house. I had our Section 8 office do a preliminary appraisal, and the going rent for my rental house was $1,050 per month. I did have several potential renters who looked at the house. Primarily, they were single income mothers with children.

Here is a hypothetical, but typical, situation. Mary is thirty-five, single with two children. She works full time as a warehouse clerk. She makes $6.00 an hour. That is $240 a week, before deductions for taxes and social security. Since she is single with children, she has to pay child care. She is responsible for feeding three mouths. HUD will take all of Mary's information and decide how much she can afford to pay in rent. Let us just say they want her to pay 10 percent of her take home pay toward rent. Her take home pay is around $200 per week. She should pay $20 a week or $80 a month toward rent. Therefore, for our house, which was approved at $1,050, Mary would pay $80 per month and HUD would direct deposit $970 into my checking account on the first of the month.

It is important to note that you may charge a deposit that is fair and equitable. In my case, the deposit was about one month's rent. Mary would need to have $1,050 for the down payment. HUD will not help with the deposit.

Yes, you can evict your tenants if they do not make their portion of the payment. But they would be losing their housing voucher benefit so it would be *really* unfortunate if they did not make their small portion of the payment. So the likelihood of this happening under Section 8 is pretty slim.

Although I did not rent to a Section 8 tenant, I was open to that option. There is no way of knowing why the prospects did not choose our property. Two prospective tenants were moving here from out of state. Two others were moving here from another part of the state, and were looking to land work first. They also asked if I was flexible on the deposit. Meaning would I take $300–$400 now and give me $100–$200 per month until I got the full deposit. This makes me wonder if the Section 8 tenants have a hard time with a large deposit. However, that may not be the case with Section 8. They may be moving from a previous rental situation, and will get that deposit back so they can pay you.

DOES YOUR HOUSE QUALIFY?

Once a prospective Section 8 tenant decides he or she wants to move in, HUD will conduct an initial inspection. They will also inspect your house annually for safe living conditions and adjust the rent for cost of living increases. What is HUD looking for? Here is a breakdown of the federal government's Basic Standards as explained in their document HUD—52580-a (20 pages). You can also search HUD documents at www.hud.gov/offices/hsg/mfh/rfp/sec8rfp.cfm.

Bedrooms

A bedroom is a room with a window, a closet, and a door. HUD requires two ways to exit a room in case of a fire. Technically, my rental house can qualify as a four-bedroom rental. The house is a split-level design, with a finished basement. The basement is one large room with vinyl tiles on the floor, paneling on the walls, and drywall on the ceiling. For entry and exit, there are the door and stairs from the main floor, the double sliding glass door, and four windows. The half bath and laundry area are also downstairs. However, the bathroom and laundry do not matter. Personally, it does not look like a bedroom to me, but it could certainly be used as one.

As it turned out, my tenants will be using it as a bedroom. I provided two plastic wardrobe closets for them to hang their clothes in. I had used them in a previous home for out-of-season clothes and was about to throw them away when we bought the rental house. One man's trash is another man's treasure!

Sanitary Facilities

A flush toilet in a separate, private room, a fixed basin with hot and cold running water, and a shower or tub with hot and cold running water shall be present in the prospective rental, all in proper operating condition. Rental maximums are based on number of bedrooms only. Therefore, a three-bedroom, two-and-a-half-bath home will be in the same category as a three-bedroom, one-bath home. The property does not have to have a washer/dryer or connections for them. You are not required to have a dishwasher.

Food Preparation and Refuse Disposal

Cooking stove or range top with either an oven or microwave and a refrigerator of appropriate size for the unit, supplied by either the landlord or the family, and a kitchen sink with hot and cold running water shall be present. Adequate space for the storage, preparation, and serving of food shall be provided. We chose to let the tenant furnish the refrigerator. However, we have an extra in our basement we would have been able to put into the rental house if necessary. If you think about what needs the most maintenance and repair in your home, it is probably appliances and the toilets. I chose to reduce the number of appliances I have to repair.

Space and security. The prospective rental must contain a living room, kitchen area, and bathroom. The prospective rental must contain at least one bedroom or living/sleeping room of appropriate size for each two persons. Persons of the opposite sex, other than husband and wife or very young children, will not be required to occupy the same bedroom or living/sleeping room. A husband and wife with a fifteen-year-old daughter, and twin twelve-year-old boys would qualify for a three-bedroom voucher. They can rent a four-bedroom if they choose, but they would receive the payment allowed for the three-bedroom unit. If they had the fifteen-year-old girl and one twelve-year-old boy, they would still qualify for a three-bedroom. Exterior doors and windows accessible from outside the unit shall be lockable.

Smoke Detector

The prospective rental shall contain a working smoke detector on every level and in an appropriate location to provide maximum warning to occupants should a fire or smoke situation occur.

Thermal Environment

The prospective rental shall contain safe heating that is in proper operating condition and provides adequate heat to each room in the prospective rental appropriate for the climate to assure a healthy living environment. Unvented space heaters that deliver enough heat to assure a healthy living environment are acceptable. To determine if the family has adequate heat during winter months, the family will be questioned regarding adequacy of heat. The American Gas Association (AGA) seal of approval must be present on each space heater in order to pass Housing Quality Standards (HQS). Calculations must be completed to determine the safety of the unvented space heater. There is no requirement for air conditioning, even in Hotlanta. I doubt you could get someone to rent your house without air conditioning, though.

Illumination and Electricity

Each room shall have adequate natural or artificial illumination to permit normal indoor activities and to support the health and safety of occupants. Living and sleeping rooms shall include at least one window. A ceiling or wall type light fixture shall be present and working in the bathroom and kitchen area. At least two electric outlets, one of which may be part of an overhead light, shall be present and operable in the living area, kitchen area, and each bedroom area. The kitchen, however, must have at least one overhead light and one working wall outlet. HUD has no requirements for ground fault circuit interrupters (GFCI outlets will shut off if shorted by water) near water sources. However, it may be required by the building code in your area.

Structure and Materials

Ceiling, walls, and floors shall not have any serious defects such as severe bulging or leaning, large holes, loose surface materials, severe buckling or noticeable movement under walking stress, missing parts or other serious damage. All floors must be covered (e.g., linoleum, carpet, rugs, hardwood sealant, paint). The roof structure shall be firm, and the roof shall be weather tight. The exterior wall structure and exterior wall surface shall not have any serious defects such as serious leaning, buckling, sagging, cracks or holes, loose siding, or other serious damage. The condition and equipment of interior and exterior stairways, halls, porches, walkways, and so on shall be such as not to present a danger of tripping or falling. All stairs with four or more steps require handrails, and porches and balconies more than 30 inches high require guardrails.

Interior Air Quality

The prospective rental shall be free from dangerous levels of air pollution from carbon monoxide, sewer gas, fuel gas, dust, and other harmful air pollutants. Air circulation shall be adequate throughout the unit. Bathroom areas shall have at least one window that opens or other adequate exhaust ventilation.

Water Supply

Either public or private sanitary water supply is acceptable. You can also be on septic tank or sewer.

Lead Based Paint

- Units that were constructed prior to 1978 and are occupied by a child younger than seven must be inspected for defective paint on all interior and exterior painted surfaces of a residential structure. If defective paint surfaces are found, correction must occur within 30 days of notification by the Department of Community Affairs (DCA) to the landlord.
- Units that were constructed prior to 1978 and are occupied by a child younger than seven with Elevated Blood Level (EBL) must receive treatment to all intact and nonintact interior and exterior painted surfaces of a residential structure.
- Units that were constructed prior to 1978 and are occupied by no minors shall have defective paint conditions included as a part of the contract rent negotiations.

Access

The unit must have a private entrance without the tenant's going through another prospective rental. An alternative means of egress from the building is required.

Site and Neighborhood

The site and neighborhood must be reasonably free of conditions that would endanger the health and safety of residents, such as dangerous walks, steps, structural instability, flooding, poor drainage, septic tank backups, excessive accumulation of trash (more than one person can pick up in an hour), vermin or rodent infestation, and/or fire hazards.

Sanitary Condition

The unit and its equipment must be free of vermin and rodent infestation.

HOW DO YOU PARTICIPATE?

"Section 8 sounds great, but how do I get started?" Here's a simple step-by-step process to get you going in the right direction:

1. You advertise your rental house in the paper with "Section 8 ok" in the ad.
2. Prospective tenants call you to view the house.
3. They view the house and fill out a credit application and pay for a credit check.
4. When they decide they want to live in your house, they call HUD and reference Section 8.
5. You, the prospective tenant, and the HUD representative, meet at the house for the inspection and signing of the lease (Use your standard lease! See Chapter 12 on lease agreements).
6. HUD collects direct deposit information for rent payments into your account.
7. The first month's rent will be paid by check and all subsequent months are direct deposited.
8. The tenant pays a security deposit.
9. The tenant moves in.
10. HUD performs annual inspection.

WHAT ARE YOUR RESPONSIBILITIES AS A SECTION 8 LANDLORD?

As the landlord, how do you ensure compliance with Section 8? HUD lists four key areas of compliance in their document HUD—5280-a.

1. **Comply with the lease.** The landlord's major responsibilities under the lease are to:

   Collect the tenant's share of the rent.
   Make timely repairs and keep the unit in good condition.

2. **Comply with all applicable federal, state and local regulations, fair housing laws, and landlord-tenant laws.**

3. **Allow unit inspections.** At least once a year, a Department of Community Affairs (DCA) representative will inspect the house to make sure that it is in good condition. The landlord should correct any deficiencies as soon as they are discovered. The DCA may defer rent increases, withhold payments, and/or terminate the Housing Assistance Payments (HAP) contract if deficiencies are not corrected. Special inspections, which may occur more than once a year, are any inspections that are not annually scheduled and/or are requested by the owner, tenants, the DCA, or HUD.

4. **Comply with the Housing Assistance Payments (HAP) contract.** The landlord must comply with all terms of the HAP contract. The landlord's major responsibilities are to:

   - Renegotiate the lease with the tenant and the DCA within the required time frame.
   - Provide the DCA representative with a copy of the eviction proceedings at the same time the tenant is informed of eviction proceedings.
   - Inform the DCA immediately of a vacancy caused by the Section 8 tenants.

So . . . You do not want to be a strong-arm rent collector? Check into the Section 8 opportunity! The advantage is you have most of your money, and possibly all of it direct deposited to your checking account on the first day of the month. The disadvantage is it may be harder to find a tenant who qualifies and has the deposit. Here are a few resources to consult for more information:

www.hud.gov/library/index.cfm
www.nhlp.org/html/sec8/index.htm
To contact your nearest HUD office see www.hud.gov/local/
  index.cfm.

MOTIVATIONAL QUOTE

Many receive advice, only the wise profit from it.
                                                    Syrus

CHAPTER 6

Finding the Right House

You have been doing your research, putting together a team, and lining up financing options. Now you need to find a rental house that is going to make you money. But with hundreds to even thousands of "for sale" properties within a 30-minute drive from your home at any given time, where do you begin your search? How do you avoid buying a dog of an investment that drains your finances instead of pushing you closer to financial independence?

Robert Kiyosaki in his book *Retire Young, Retire Rich* talks about a friend of his who came to him all excited about buying her first rental property—right near the beach in San Diego. Out of curiosity, Kiyosaki probed a little deeper. "How many properties did you look at?" he asked. She replied she had looked at only two—both within the same complex—before buying the one. Seemed easy enough, right?

Well, one year later, this once excited investor was losing about $460 per month and was destined to call it quits with rental properties. What happened? Here is the rundown:

First, the homeowners association raised the monthly maintenance fee, an increase she did not expect. The number of potential good rental condominiums as a ratio of total condominiums for sale is fairly low. Let us look at the advantages of a condominium over an apartment for a potential renter. A condominium is often much like an apartment. Families like to rent houses for several reasons. The yard is great for children. There is more privacy in a single family home. And it is the American Dream. It may not be home ownership, but it looks like it to everyone who drives by. The condominium concept may be attractive to those of you who do not want to deal with maintenance. But be careful with this type of home. Many homeowners associations in our area are limiting the percent of occupants that can be nonowners. The reason—liability insurance. The insurance company feels too many renters would mean less concern for the property. You do not want to buy a great deal only to find out you are not allowed to rent the unit. Condominiums also have association fees to consider. Yes, it is a more carefree experience, but you pay for it! Weigh all three of these issues (the advantage over an apartment, you may not be allowed to rent it right away, and you have high maintenance fees) before you venture into the condominium business.

Second, the investor did not know how much rent she could *actually* collect. Come to find out, the market rate was much lower than she had anticipated. That is a big, big mistake. So how do you know what rent you can charge? There are several ways. The Sunday local newspaper is a great way. Since I live in a large metropolitan area, our paper is divided by area of town, then by city. I looked at rental property mainly in the county in which I once lived and with which I was very familiar. I checked the rent sections of those areas of town. Many advertisers give a general idea of where the home is by adding the school district, neighborhood, or main road. Remember the Section 8 information. Call your local contact to get his/her opinion on what HUD would approve. In my experience, HUD has been very open to talking with me. Unfortunately, the HUD agent was often hard to reach, because she was in the office only one day per week. Next time you are riding through the neighborhood looking for properties for sale, do not overlook the rent signs. Take down the phone number and call them. Find out about the house. How many bedrooms and baths does it have? Does it have a refrigerator? Is there a basement? Find out the length of the lease and what they need for a deposit. Are they including any utilities? Just remember when you get calls on your property, you may get the same calls. Personally, I do not mind another landlord calling for information. Your mentors can be very helpful if they also have property in the same area. What about that real estate investment club—someone there should know. *Wow*, there are sources everywhere if you just look around. It is important to note that your appraiser can also provide you with an estimate of what local rents are.

Lastly, when she tried to sell the property, the agent discovered that she had paid $25,000 more than market value, putting her in a serious financial crunch. I do not know about you, but I cannot afford a $25,000 mistake. I cannot stress enough that you need to have a team that is knowledgeable in the business of rental property and in real estate locations. This includes you. You are the main part of your team. Do your research. Forget watching that rerun on television. Get on the Internet and look at real estate for sale. Buy a Sunday subscription to your weekend newspaper and go over it with a fine-tooth comb. Look for houses for sale and houses for rent. Get into your car and go ride around.

The moral? Do your homework before you buy. Had she known about these issues ahead of time, the buyer would have certainly passed on the property and kept looking.

This is precisely why this chapter is so important. While no investment strategy is entirely risk-free, if you know what a moneymaking house looks like, you stand a much greater chance for success. Here's a framework to help you select a money-making property in a way that minimizes your risks and maximizes potential rewards!

BECOME AN EXPERT ON LOCATION

As the real estate cliché goes, when it comes to buying rental houses, think location, location, and location! No matter how good a deal you can strike on a rental home, if no one wants to live in that neighborhood or there is not the right infrastructure for attracting renters, your investment could cost you—a lot!

I have friends who bought a rental property several months ago in a one stoplight little town about an hour's drive from downtown Atlanta. They have yet to find a solid long-term renter. They get three to six month tenants but it sits empty one to two months per year, so they are losing quite a bit of money each year. Why are they having a difficult time? Location, location, location. They are discovering that a town with one traffic light is not exactly a great source of jobs. And without a lot of companies bringing jobs to the town, you are going to have a pretty small pool of potential renters to choose from. The fall of 2002 was also the hardest time in 20 years to rent a house. Interest rates have been so low for so long that anybody who could afford a house, bought one. Developers are also building apartment complexes because interest rates are so low—so right now we have an oversupply of rental housing. Once the economy picks up and interest rates go back up, we will probably see the rental market get back in balance. We have also had the most liberal approval guidelines, thus generating higher foreclosures rates that will generate tighter approval guidelines—see a cycle here?! These tighter approval guidelines will drive the rental market back up. From the time I write this book to the time it gets to your store's bookshelf, we could be in a dramatically different economy. But business cycles repeat themselves.

So how do you educate yourself on the location? As I mentioned before, get "hands on" and spend time driving through and studying the area.

A Checklist to Guide Your Analysis

How is the neighborhood kept up?   Do people take good care of their homes and yards, or do many of the homes look neglected? Check how many cars are parked in the driveway and in the street. If this is a neighborhood with many cars, it could have multiple families per house. Ideally, you want one family in your house. Are there as many cars in the daytime as the evenings and on weekends? You want a working class neighborhood. When you narrow down your search to a few areas or houses, check the neighborhood at those different times. It may look terrific on Tuesday at one o'clock in the afternoon, yet you want to lock your door at eight o'clock on a Saturday evening. Ask yourself, would a renter be comfortable to live in this neighborhood?

What support services and amenities are in close proximity?   Here you are looking for shopping centers, grocery stores, parks, jogging trails, and other amenities that would be attractive to renters. If available, it is a plus to have access to the metropolitan transit system. My first rental house is located about a block from a major grocery store chain and a bus stop.

How desirable is the school system?   "Which schools would my children attend" is usually one of the first questions I get about the house. You can find out the info on the school systems by contacting the schools, your realtor, or your realtor's web site. My rental house is in one of the largest and most reputable county school systems in the state. All but one of my prospective renters had school age children. This is a very powerful draw for most parents. It is also important to know if the local school has any after school care available. That is another selling point to the working parent.

Are there safe places for children to play? How are the sidewalks? Are there playgrounds nearby? Or does the property itself have a fenced-in yard? Parents are looking for the peace of mind that their children will be safe at play. Most of my potential renters were parents moving from an apartment or another area of the state to improve the quality of life for their family. Look for houses that would make a good home. Look with the eyes of a parent. What is in it for them?

How convenient is the house located from interstate and other main arteries? Most renters just like me, do not want to spend more time than they have to driving to work. If your house can minimize that drive time, you strengthen your leverage in landing tenants. My house is located about two miles from one of the major interstates that run through the city. The renter can be on a four-lane highway in about five minutes. They can be on I-285, which circles the city, in about eight minutes. That was a major selling point for me with this house. It is also on a two-lane main artery. There are advantages and disadvantages to this. The advantage is its visibility when it is time to rent. Many people see the sign in front of the house. It also makes for easier directions to the house. If it is too difficult to find, you will have your prospect simply give up and go somewhere else. The disadvantage is there is more traffic in front of the house. A potential renter with small children may be concerned for safety. Fortunately, this house also has a fenced yard, which enhances the safety factor.

What are the going rental rates? You have done your research, so now you have a clear, realistic idea of what you can charge for rent. Therefore, you can work backwards to determine whether buying a particular property would be profitable. (I show you how to do this later in the chapter.)

Where does the house stand in terms of property taxes? Property taxes, in conjunction with several other factors, affect what you should charge for rent. So do not get blindsided. Contact the county tax office and find out what the millage rate is for the property. They can also tell you what the taxes were last year on the property, and what value that was based on. Some areas will base your home value on what you paid for the property. And homeowners tax exemptions are not available on rental homes, so do not try to estimate from the taxes on your personal home. I have lived in two counties in Georgia and they do homeowners exemptions differently. Call the county offices of any county you are interested in. The booklets lined up at the exit of the super-market that list homes for sale often have the tax information listed. You can also check on the Internet and with your real estate agent.

What are the costs due to membership to homeowners association (HOA)? These costs impact your expenses, so know exactly where you stand before you buy. Be certain the real estate agent checks on this for you. The property listing does not always give the correct information. My personal residence is in a neighborhood that charges a $1,000 initiation fee. A neighborhood with swimming and tennis will cost around $360 a year or more, and most are not optional. It is not a large sum, but it is an additional $30 a month out of your profit. On the up side, it may assist in attracting a renter.

What utilities are available? I personally look for properties with access to city water and city sewerage versus a well and septic tank system. This is really a maintenance cost issue for me. Friends, who own seven rental houses, have taught me from their own experience. They have had to replace three septic tanks in different houses, costing them $3,000 each. You reduce your maintenance cost exposure by buying properties with city water and sewerage. The monthly bill for water and sewerage may be higher, but if you play your cards right, you will not be paying those bills.

Is the property close to you?   This is especially important for your first rental house. You are dealing with a lot of new, unexpected issues. By living within a 15–30 minute drive from your rental house, you will be better positioned to know the market and attend to renter problems more quickly. You will also be able to go home if you forgot a key tool you needed for the day. And your wife and kids can stop by to bring you lunch! It may also be easier to find help in an area where you know people. My first rental home happened to be located within 10 minutes of my church.

OTHER CONSIDERATIONS

Look to Buy the House at Least 20 Percent below Market Value

Now when I look at houses, I am looking for a three-bedroom, two-bath house that I can get into for much less than $125,000. I am trying to get into the $60,000 to $90,000 price range. Although I made good money on my first deal, my ultimate goal is for each individual house to stand financially on its own merit—in other words, none of my money in the deal. If I can get each house to finance itself, then I can buy an unlimited amount of houses. I do not want to have to use the equity in my current home for permanent down payment financing. If I had $10,000 to invest and used $5,000 for a down payment, I would be able to buy only two houses now. I would be out of down payment capital after the second house. I may have to use temporary financing of an equity line of credit out of my current home, but I do not want to have to use it permanently. If I have to buy the house with a down payment from my equity line, I want to be able to refinance the loan and get my down payment back. Then, I can continue to use that equity line over and over again. There are 100 different ways to finance a house and this is just my first one, so please consider the fact that you may find a better situation than I have presented.

Focus on Houses Most Appealing to The Widest Renter Market

Previously, I mentioned several books I have read and seminars I have attended. Some of those authors/speakers say it is best to buy a three-bedroom, two-bath house. Nobody wants a three-bedroom, one-bath—they are very difficult to rent. Some people say it is very difficult to rent a two-bedroom, one-bath. It is much better to get a two-bedroom, two-bath. Some people like to rent condominiums, and others like to do multiunit projects, such as a duplex or quadruplex because they have economies of scale. In other words all four units are all right there together. However, most will agree that the single-family residential three-bedroom, two-bath house is the most popular rental unit on the market today. People who are trying to get out of apartments and want a house are looking for that combination. Therefore, I focus on three-bedroom, two-bath houses. A lady came to a garage sale several years ago who rented furnished houses. She bought the furniture and bedding at garage sales and flea markets—she was primarily renting to people in corporate and divorce situations. She put a couple of hundred dollars of yard sale furniture into a house and got a couple of hundred dollars a month higher rent. She also had a happy little grin on her face as she told us the story.

I considered furnishing my rental house for a while, but decided against it, simply because more people are looking to move from one place to another. If they are already living in one location, they will likely have furniture and personal belongings to move. However, if you have a place you are having trouble renting, this might be the ticket. Check your local paper for how many furnished homes are on the market. This could be a way to eliminate your competition. There are niches in the market, so if you have a condominium, this could be the perfect solution to set it apart from an apartment. In the case of a divorce, the spouse may have left with no furniture and may not want a yard to maintain, either. This could put a smile on your face, too!

ANALYZE THE CASH-FLOW OPPORTUNITY

Can you generate positive cash flow on the rental property? Once you know what you can reasonably charge for rent, you can then run the numbers to determine whether or not the deal would be a money-maker for you.

For example, in the area where I bought my first home, a three-bedroom house, under Section 8, would pay as much as $1,150 per month—according to market conditions and comparables. Of $1,150 rental income, I can run the numbers, working backwards to determine that if I can get roughly a $125,000 mortgage for 30 years at 7 percent interest and with taxes, insurance, and so forth, they will cost me about $1,050 a month. If I do a Section 8 for $1,150, I can have $100 a month positive cash flow.

When I first started, I made a simple worksheet sheet like this.

Total or Annual Amount

$_____	Equity line on current house	Monthly pmt $_____
$_____	Bank loan	Monthly pmt $_____
$_____	Taxes	Monthly pmt $_____
$_____	Homeowners insurance	Monthly pmt $_____
$_____	Private mortgage insurance	Monthly pmt $_____
$_____	Maintenance	Monthly pmt $_____
$_____	Advertising	Monthly pmt $_____
$_____	Vacancy factor	Monthly pmt $_____
$_____	Total	Monthly pmt $_____

Equity Line

I would write down how much I was going to take out of my equity line of credit on my house, say $5,000, and how much the monthly payment would cost. That was perhaps $20 a month. In the fall of

2002, I got an interest-only equity line for 4.7 percent annual inter-est rate, which is the current prime rate. The calculation for that monthly payment goes like this: $5,000 × .0475/12 = $19.79. The outstanding balance is $5,000, .0475 is the calculator entry for 4.75 percent annual interest, and 12 is the number of months in a year, so .0475/12 is the amount of interest payable each month. An equity line of credit is also available that is a revolving line of credit. It works more like your credit card. I choose interest only because I planned on having the rental house pay it off. This gives me the lowest payment in slow months and the ability to make large repay-ments to principal in good months.

Bank Loan

Then, I would get the bank loan for the rest of the money. I would write down the balance and what the monthly payment would be. You need to have a financial calculator or an interest rate payment calculation table to figure amortized loans. There are several web sites available for you to find these items. I have also included a table in the appendix you can use to ballpark payments. My favorite reference desk web site is www.refdesk.com. This web site merely lists all the links to just about anything you can imagine. I have started many projects at that site.

Here are some mortgage calculation web sites.

http://www.quoteserv.com/mortgage/calculator.shtml
http://www.hsh.com/calc-amort.html
http://ray.met.fsu.edu/~bret/amortize.html

Taxes

Call your local taxing authority for property tax rates. In my case I was buying in a county that I had lived in for 10 years so I was familiar with the tax rate. Many times the real estate listing will tell you what the property taxes will cost. You must remember that you are *not* going to have the homestead exemption for property taxes on your rental house. If you are used to paying $1,200, it might cost as much as $1,600 without the homestead exemption. The homestead exemption is a tax reduction for property owners who live in the house. In other words landlords pay more property taxes than nonlandlords. "Hey, wait, I thought we were getting into real estate to get lower taxes!" Remember, you are letting the tenant pay the tax bill. This gets back to the homework again. Homestead exemption varies from county to county. It is much larger in the county we live in now than where we moved from.

Homeowners Insurance

You have to have homeowners insurance to protect your house against fire, and other damages. Some people call this hazard insurance—same thing. You want to talk to your insurance agent about the difference between owner occupied, investor, builder's risk, vacancy, and umbrella policies. This is not a book on insurance but you should know that each company is a little different on how they calculate replacement costs and what is included in each type of policy. Talk to your agent. Better yet—talk to three agents. Now let us get back to homeowners insurance. On a $135,000 house in Georgia, I paid about $470 per year. Renters insurance is something totally different and it is purchased by the tenant to protect his belongings. In the case where a tornado hit the neighborhood, a tree fell on the house, and rain came in and caused damage—the landlord's homeowners insurance would fix the house. The tenant's renters insurance would pay for their furniture or other belongings that were destroyed. The landlord is not liable for the rain damaged Philips 42" high definition widescreen television with surround sound. Get the tenants to buy renters insurance—it is pretty cheap; I have been quoted between $150 and $225 per *year*. I included a recommendation for renters insurance in my lease. That way, the renter cannot say they thought I was responsible for their personal belongings.

Mortgage Insurance or PMI—Private Mortgage Insurance

PMI protects the lender only and you pay for it. It is mandatory on single mortgage loans over 80 percent of the value of the house. Some banks offer combination or piggyback loans to avoid PMI. That is where the homeowner puts 10 percent down, gets an 80 percent first mortgage and then a 10 percent second mortgage. Talk to your mortgage banker about this option. My final mortgage loan amount was $125,000 and my PMI was $96 per month. I talk more about PMI in Chapter 8.

Total Payment

When I added all those numbers up, they totaled $1,050 on a $125,000 mortgage on a house that had been appraised for $139,000.

Advertising Costs

You also need to add in advertising costs. In the Atlanta area, it costs about $100 per weekend to advertise a house for rent in the major newspaper. If you are going to advertise for six weeks, that is $600. You must add those numbers to your costs. There are other ways to advertise your house, also. You can print flyers and post them at the local businesses. Many supermarkets have bulletin boards for customers to post things for sale or rent. Even though I advertised in the large metropolitan newspaper, the house rented from the sign in the yard. I bought a nice HOUSE FOR RENT sign for the yard and attached a tube that holds flyers. The tube lasted less than a week. I have no idea what happened to it, and it was not replaced. The sign is now waiting for my next deal.

Vacancy Factor

You also want to add into your numbers a vacancy factor of one or two months a year. If you have a one-year tenant and he/she moves out at the end of the term—how quickly can you get people back into that house? It might be worth a $200 fee to your existing tenants if they can provide replacements—which you obviously get to approve. Fortunately, if your tenant does not fulfill the term of the lease, you will be able to keep the deposit.

Ongoing Maintenance Costs

If you have a one-year lease, it will take you one week or two weeks to get the house cleaned up, repainted, and advertised before the next people move in. Your ultimate goal is to have long-term tenants—people who stay for several years. Long-term tenants reduce your advertising, vacancy, painting, and carpet cleaning expenses. Carpet cleaning will average about $300, and three cans of paint and some roller covers total about $60. Do not buy cheap paint—it takes more coats, and thus more time, to get the desired finish. As soon as I have the formula for the perfect long-term tenant, I will be writing the book *How to Find the Perfect Tenant*. I do not recommend you wait for this book to hit the presses to make your move in real estate!

Evaluate Properties with Rehab Costs in Mind

Trying to calculate rehab costs reminds me of a story of when I was a boat mechanic at a marina during my high school and college summers. I spent some of my spring breaks going to classes in Milwaukee, Wisconsin, and Waukegan, Illinois, learning additional skills in repairing outboard motors. One of the engineers who taught our class related a story about his job when he was in the military. His job was as a demolitions expert. Since he was an engineer, his job was to measure the walls of a building and calculate how much dynamite it would take to blow up the building. Once he did all of his calculations on how much dynamite it would take, he would double the amount of the explosives just to make sure he got the job done.

When you come to rehab projects, you are going to find a very similar concept. It takes twice as long and costs twice as much as you originally think. We talk more about this in Chapter 9. My brother, the architect, refers to it as the "fudge factor." He and I have done several projects around our homes, have done careful calculations on bar napkins, and then have added in a $2,000 or $3,000 "fudge factor" for all the things we did not think of. You can buy a lot of fudge with my "fudge factor"!

I am going to paint the trim in the bedrooms the same color as the walls because it is faster. I can patch small holes in the walls, ceilings, doors and so on, but I have to know that the house itself is structurally sound. You will want to develop a relationship, or meet an inspector, who cannot only inspect your houses, but also teach you what to look for, so that when you are out shopping for houses, you have a basic understanding of what to look for.

I had met a real estate agent at a previous seminar who told me about a house that was not on the market yet. When I went out to look at it, it had cracks all along the foundation in the back corner. I had no interest in a house with cracked foundation walls. It just looked unsafe. You want to be able to determine early if it is a structural problem or a cosmetic problem. This is a skill you develop over time by looking at houses. You must be able to tell the difference. After you buy four or five houses and build some experience, you might take on more structural problems, but you will need to get compensated for them accordingly.

We go into more detail in Chapter 9 about where to spend your money on rehab.

Exterior and Interior Considerations

When I look at a house, I am looking for something that is going to have very low maintenance. I want something that has brick, vinyl siding, aluminum siding—something that is not going to need to be painted. My first rental house had a poured concrete wall foundation with yellow aluminum siding. It had a lot of mold on it since it had not been pressure washed in years. All I had to do was pressure wash that aluminum siding, and it looked brand new again. Look for the type of house that is going to have very little outside mainte- nance. You want a house that has a good concrete foundation and driveway so you do not have to spend big dollars repairing them. I like houses that are on sewers rather than septic tanks, and I like them to be on city water rather than a well. I want as many things without maintenance as I can.

I like to have a house that has a reasonably new roof and a rea- sonably new furnace and air-conditioning system, or I want a much lower sales price so I can factor those costs into the equation. I also prefer a gas hot water heater. By doing research, I find that most tenants, and most homeowners, prefer a gas range. Gas ranges have fewer problems than electric ranges, even though Home Depot and Lowe's are now selling replacement parts for electric ranges. The extra bonus you get from a gas range is that when the power goes out in a winter storm, you can still cook food on a gas range. Gas ranges are cheaper to buy than electric ranges. My house had such a filthy gas stove, I just threw it into the dumpster. We went out and replaced it with a new stove from the scratch and dent store for less than $200. It did not have digital controls nor was it a self-cleaning model. Nan and I discussed whether we should pay extra for the self-cleaning feature. When we learned the brand new oven was only $200, we decided to drop the self-cleaning option. You never know if the tenant will take care of the appliances, so why spend more than you need to?

SUMMARY

These are some of the things that you want to be looking for:

- Aluminum siding, vinyl siding or brick. Any combination of low-maintenance siding.
- Solid driveways, sidewalks, and foundations.

- Good roof.
- Good furnaces.
- Air-conditioners that will not need to be replaced within the next five years. There are areas that may not need air-conditioning. However, Georgia is not one of them.
- Gas hot water heaters.
- Modern, good-looking appliances.
- Some problem that is easily cured but appears to be a problem. For example, purple walls need only paint; carpet that smells of pet odor or cigarette smoke needs only to be steam cleaned or replaced. You will notice yourself using the terms "it needs carpet and paint" a lot.

If we could find a perfect house, it would not be on sale so do not expect that everything will look pretty when you go out looking for your first rental house. Whatever is missing from the perfect list should be reflected in the sales price. I once heard one of my mentors say he loved to walk into a house that smelled of pet urine. Why? An experienced real estate agent will tell you the potential buyer never makes it five feet past the front door. Buyers are so turned off by the odor, they do not care what the house looks like, they do not want to live there. Generally speaking, home buyers have no creativity when looking at a house. It is hard for them to picture what the house could look like with new paint and their furniture. This means you will have less competition for these properties. Stick a little perfume under your nose, and go house hunting!

HOME INSPECTIONS

Home inspections by a properly trained person can save you a small fortune. They can show you the difference between what needs to be repaired and what needs to be avoided. You should be able to attend and walk through the house with the inspector. You can watch how he inspects your house to give you tips on doing a preliminary inspection of your own deals. I like to ask the inspector questions about maintenance.

- Should I reinforce the railing on the deck?
- Does this termite damage look like more than a cosmetic problem?
- How can I fix that leaky gutter?
- Where do I turn off the water supply to the house?

If you search on the Internet for Home Inspection you will find more hits than you will ever need in a lifetime. By reading several of these sites and spending time (and money) with a couple of different inspectors, I put together a list of top 10 things to look for when inspecting a house.

1. Look up. When most people walk into a room, they look at the carpet and the walls. Remember to look at the ceiling. That is where you will see the telltale sign of a **leaking roof**. When you approach the house, look at the shingles. Good shingles lie flat. Bad shingles have the edges turned up or even have missing pieces. Your roof may in good shape but you still have a water mark developing on your master bedroom ceiling (can you tell I've been here?!). You need to inspect the plumbing vent pipes that come up through the roof. Each one of those has a boot that is to seal around the pipe— they dry rot in the hot Georgia sun. A good rainstorm will let water drip down along the outside of those vent pipes and rot the drywall or support structure.
2. Other sources of water damage can come from **faulty plumbing**. The most common are old or incompatible piping materials. Faulty fixtures can drip into a cabinet, causing it to rot, and then drip onto the floor causing it also to rot. It is amazing how much destruction can be caused by a little drip of water. When I do home repairs, I get more frustrated with plumbing problems than with most anything else be-

cause of that one last little pesky drip of water. Electrical outlets do not drip electricity—they either work or they do not! I have had good success using Teflon tape on anything with threads to help form a good leakproof seal.

3. Examples of a **poorly maintained home** include cracked or peeling paint, crumbling masonry, plumbing fixtures that leak, electrical fixtures that have shoddy or faulty wiring. Sometimes you will find fixtures that are loose and wobbly and just need to be tightened up with a screwdriver or wrench. I like to look at the back deck. If a homeowner pressure washed and sealed his deck every couple of years, it will look great. If he neglected this boring and labor-intensive duty, he probably neglected other things, too. If he did not pressure wash and seal the deck, it will be rotting, stained, and have a loose railing. Decks are not cheap; do the required maintenance.

4. A poorly maintained home can also lead to **minor structural damage**. This means that the house still has a long life expectancy but it needs some repairs. These may be to rotting windows, sagging rafters, rotting floor joists, and so on. What do all these things have in common? Water damage. Deal with the problem while it is cheap because it will not go away and it will only get more expensive as time goes on.

5. The water damage in #4 can start around windows and doors so **check the exterior** of the house. Many times you can repair the problem with caulk and weather stripping. By reducing the drafts around windows and doors, you will also lower your heating and cooling costs, which brings me to my next item.

6. **Heating and cooling systems** or HVAC (heating, venting, air-conditioning). The HVAC has a life of about 15 years so if you are looking at a house that is 12 years old you need to know that you are looking at a pretty good expense in a couple of years. Two of the biggest problems with a faulty HVAC are:

- The furnace can put toxic carbon monoxide fumes into your home.
- The furnace can quit in the coldest part of the winter and all the plumbing pipes will freeze. When they melt, they can burst and pour water throughout your house causing major damage.

7. While you are checking out the HVAC system, be sure to have the **ventilation** checked out. Poor ventilation can result in too much moisture in the house causing problems with interior walls and structural elements. Poor ventilation can also contribute to allergic reactions.

8. A common topic with inspectors is the **outside drainage** system. I have had three houses inspected and we always start with a curbside look at the house and discuss how the lot is graded. To improve drainage, you may have to repair or install gutters and downspouts. In extreme cases you may have to regrade the lot to channel water away from the house.

9. In older homes a common problem is **faulty or outdated wiring.** If you have a home office with computers, fax machines, laser printers, and the like, you may have to have some additional circuits added to your system. You can buy a $5 tester that you plug into your electrical outlets to determine if they are connected properly.

10. As soon as you walk into the house, turn on the **appliances.** Run the dishwasher, flush the toilets, turn on the HVAC system, and so on. These items take time to go through their cycles and you can look at other rooms while waiting on them.

HOUSES WE DID NOT BUY AND WHY

As I said earlier in Chapter 4, we did not just wake up one day and decide to buy a rental house. This has been an ongoing project, and since we always like to look at houses anyway—we were always on the lookout for a good deal. Here are some stories of the houses we did not buy and why.

Condo/House

We were searching the Internet for houses in our selected area, searching by price range with three bedrooms. We came across a "house" that looked like a condominium. Sure enough on inspection we found a brand new subdivision of condominiums. You could buy one unit at a time (compared to buying a four-unit quadruplex). The developer had an association that took care of cutting the grass and maintaining the pool. We did not like the schools and when we drove through the subdivision, we noticed that most of the cars were parked outside the garage. While inspecting the different floor plans, we noticed a lack of storage space and realized that people were using their garage as an attic and parking their cars in the driveway. It made the complex look very cluttered. We also did not like the fact that the buildings had been built right on top of each other. Not only did you have a next-door neighbor but you had another neighbor 40 feet off your back door. In some cases the back decks were only 10 feet from each other. One good family quarrel might get as many as five or six families talking! It was a brand new condominium so it came with a warranty, which we liked. The warranty would cover most repair costs for the first year, and the association fees would get us out of the maintenance business forever. Since the units were selling like hotcakes, the developer was not negotiating on the price. That meant there would be no cash out at closing, only cash in. Cash in was one of the reasons to pass on this house. The other was the uncertainty of how the neighborhood would hold up. And a big factor in the decision was the gut feeling that said "no thanks."

Weird House

We got a call from a realtor that he was listing a foreclosure that needed work. This was a situation where my real estate agent called us before there was even a sign in the yard. I knew about this only because of my relationship with the real estate agent. He told us that the house had termites in the past, which had caused some damage so the house needed to be repaired. As we drove through the neighborhood we noticed very few FOR SALE signs and no rental signs. The houses for the most part were well-maintained and did not have cars up on blocks or old appliances sitting out in the yard. Therefore, the neighborhood was a winner. We dropped by and wandered through the house. The missing siding by the front door made inspection easy—the termites had done some damage. The house turned us off because it had a strange floor plan. The kitchen was in a little alcove with no windows and very little counter space. It felt like a cave. The master bedroom had the sinks right out in the bedroom so if your spouse woke up early to go to work, you would be awake, too. The back wall of the house had wood siding right down to the ground level, and I was afraid that termites had gotten up in there, too, and just had not been discovered. One of the bays in the garage had been converted to a bedroom and the back screened porch was only accessible through the garage. The back screened porch was a poorly constructed addition and the wood had rotted. The whole porch needed to be removed. We passed. The list price on this house was around $95,000. Oddly enough, it sold for more than list price. Someone out there was willing to pay more to take on the risk. Not this investor! This is a great example of location, location, location. Why else would someone pay more for a house with so many serious problems?

Manufactured House

I met with one mortgage broker who thought he was God's gift to the mortgage business. He suggested we buy new manufactured homes for the rental market. He could "get us a deal." Turned out he charged astronomical rates for his "great deals." But he did bring us to consider using manufactured housing. Companies are now building regular houses in factories and bringing them out on trucks one big preconstructed chunk at a time. A typical 3-bedroom two-story house might come out in four pieces. They have a *huge* crane that puts them into place and then a crew who take about 30 days to finish the project. Once inside you cannot tell it apart from a stick-built onsite house. We just could not find the deal we were looking for. We had spent too much time chasing that concept.

HUD House

One Saturday while shopping in a small town about 15 minutes north of our house, we decided to take the back roads tour of the area. It was not long before we had found some houses in our target market. As we drove through this little neighborhood without finding a single FOR SALE or FOR RENT sign, I suddenly called out, "Whoa—house for sale—sign in the window not in the yard." Upon closer inspection it was a HUD house foreclosure. Off the front door I got the name and phone number of the agency selling it. We looked in the windows and saw hardwood floors that desperately needed to be refinished, bedrooms that had bare wood floors that needed carpet, and the kitchen with a real nice 1970s lime green countertop. The outside of the house was four sides brick—the perfect rental house due to its low maintenance. The four corners of the house had leaking gutters that had rotted the overhangs in those areas. They would obviously need some immediate attention. I probably would have also removed the gutters for good so I would not have the problem in the future. The problem with that house was that it had already been sold to a new buyer. We were too late.

The Lost House

We found a house that was listed incorrectly, or was not listed, in the multiple listing service. In this case using normal search parameters the real estate agents could not find it. My wife found it while searching a specific small real estate firm's web site. From the outside it was a nice three-bedroom two-bath split-level house with a two-car garage. The house across the street was up for sale for $15,000 more than this house. We thought we had found a house that had been overlooked and maybe no one had made any offers on. It felt like it was time to make a lowball offer. It turned out that someone had driven through the neighborhood and had made a full price offer on the house.

MOTIVATIONAL QUOTES

I do not think there is any other quality so essential to success of any kind as the quality of perseverance. It overcomes almost everything, even nature.

John D. Rockefeller

Opportunities? They are all around us . . . there is power lying latent everywhere waiting for the observant eye to discover it.

Orison Swett Marden

CHAPTER 7

A House versus a Home

THE DIFFERENCE BETWEEN A HOUSE AND A HOME

My family and I live in a home. I bought a rental house as an investment. My home is treated like a home. My rental house is treated like a business. You want your tenant to treat your house as their home. A house is a building; a home is where you live.

If you are going to have rental houses, you need to understand that it is going to take some time to manage the house, to show it, and to maintain it. You have to be willing to put in some time to your business to make sure it is profitable. But you do not want to put too much time into it, or it will pay you less than minimum wage!

In this chapter, we want to talk about how to run the business

---

The author is not an attorney or a CPA and does not intend to give legal or tax advice. You should seek competent advice from lawyers and CPAs.

side of a rental house. We cover some legal aspects and some accounting aspects.

The Legal Side

When I was doing my research, I went to places like John Adams at www.money99.com and purchased his landlord program. I also went to a web site called www.nolo.com. It has a very interesting article on the 10 tips for being a successful landlord. These are simple suggestions to help your business and your relationships with tenants run smoothly.

Do not rent to anyone before checking his or her credit history, references and possible criminal background.   One of the biggest tenant problems you will have is with those who have played the system and know how the eviction system works better than you do. They are looking for the easy marks. The first sign of an easy mark is not requiring criminal background checks and credit reports. Several reputable companies are available who will do a background check, credit report, and verify tenants income and their rent history with their previous landlord. I use a service called Heinsite Services available at www.heinsite.com, as they are in my local area. Several firms operate nationwide. Ask your mentor or someone on your team whom they suggest. I would also recommend doing a search on the Internet. The prices are all comparable. If you have problems with one when you are starting out, you might have the tenant pay $35 to one service, and you pay your own $35 to hire a second service, and compare the two. See who gets more information on your prospective tenant. Which report is the easier to use? Who was more responsive to your time frame? When I run an ad in the newspaper, I have the prospective tenant call a telephone number that will give selected information about the property. I always include the directions and general style of the house including the number of bedrooms, baths, and living areas. Anything of special interest to set apart your house? For example, if it has just been painted; the carpets have been steam cleaned; it has a fenced yard and so on. In that message I state that it is $1,050 a month to rent the house, a $1,000 security deposit, and a $35 application fee for their credit report and criminal background check. They know up front I am going to check it. If they know you are going to check credit and background criminal reports, it will tend to keep the experts from wasting their time with you. They are going to look for the easy mark where someone advertises that there is no credit check. You must do background checks. And you should have the tenant pay for it. Someone who is truly interested in your house will not bat an eye at a $35 application fee. After all, apartments charge application fees; why wouldn't you? I handed out a couple of applications and was told they would send it back with a check. Well, that never happened. I received the application fee from three potential renters, all three qualified for the house. I gave out seven applications.

Get all the important terms of the tenancy in writing.   You must be certain that your rental contract is very precise. I got mine from John Adams. It is two to three pages long in very small print, and it covers everything. When you go to use a rental contract, you need to spend time, and maybe even some money, to be sure it is very specific on every point—including a move-in inspection, a move-out inspection, what you are responsible for, and what you are *not* responsible for. Be sure the tenants get their own renters insurance and tell them what you will cover and what you will not cover. Your rental contract needs to follow your state's guidelines. Here is yet another opportunity for a mentor's advice!

Establish a clear, fair system of setting, collecting, holding, and returning security deposits.   This is where your pre move-in inspection is going to be very important. Some people use a video camera so if they have to go to court years later, they have hard evidence. Include the ceilings, floors, and walls to show their condition. When tenants move out, walk through (preferably with the tenant) and inspect the house. You will have normal wear and tear. If there are children, expect to have crayon marks on the walls. Do not worry about crayon marks. You will probably repaint between tenants. Instead, be more concerned with holes in the walls. Be more worried about the mechanicals such as the hot water heater, the furnace, and that all appliances are intact. The house should be clean when tenants move in, and clean when they move out.

Stay on top of repairs and maintenance needs. Make repairs as requested. If the property is not kept in good repair, you will alienate good tenants. They may have the right to withhold rent and sue for any injuries caused by defective conditions, or move out without notice. Find maintenance issues when they are at the fifty-cent level rather than at the five hundred dollar level. In other words, you want to be checking the caulking around the bathtub before the floor gets rotted out! Stay on top and do the simple maintenance items early. If you have a faucet that leaks, fix it earlier rather than later. (By the way, that applies to your car and your home as well; the sooner you catch maintenance problems, the cheaper it is to fix them. Remember the old Fram Oil Filter ad: "You can pay me now or pay me later"?) Also, keep a log on the house so in case you ever have to go to court, you can say to the judge that on each specific date you did this, and on this date you did that. You want to be able to show the judge the maintenance that you performed on the house to let him know that you were taking care of the property. Not only do you want to take care of it, but also you want to keep a log or a spreadsheet that documents what you did and the date it was completed. I have also hired a "spy." I have chosen to pay the exterminator myself. This is an expense a tenant might not want to pay for. To eliminate a bug or rodent infestation, I cover the exterminator. He makes quarterly visits. Sometimes he does the rental house on the same day he does my home. Since I pay the bill, I will always ask him about the condition of the house.

Do not let your tenants or property be easy marks for a criminal. You can be liable for the tenant's losses, so you need to have proper insurance. Talk to your insurance agent about the types of insurance you need for your property. Be certain that the step-down off the back deck is easy and that you have lights available on the outside because that will tend to keep criminals away. You want to make sure all of your outside light bulbs are in working order. Anything you can do to make certain your property is safe such as handrails on the outside steps and lights for security will be to your advantage. My rental house is wired for a security system. Although it is up to the tenant to activate the service, the option is available. When we first looked at this house, the back sliding door would not lock. Therefore, anyone could have come in at any time. The house did not appear to have any damage or vandalism. At that point, we knew the neighborhood was safe.

Respect your tenants' privacy.   Always notify your tenants whenever you plan to enter the rental unit, and provide as much notice as possible. Generally, 24 hours is good notice, unless of course if there is an emergency and you think the tenants might be in danger. If you just barge in unjustifiably you will alienate them. You might have an understanding that you are going to stop by once a month to replace the filter on the furnace, or let them know when the pest control person will be there. You might have him call them directly to schedule an appointment. You do want to come in to casually inspect the house. Quarterly, you can change the filter on the furnace. While there you can look around, particularly at the bathrooms and the kitchen. These are the places where you will have dripping water pipes, leaky sinks, or leaky toilets. You need to let the tenants know that you are looking for needed maintenance, and you do not care if they have a pile of clothes sitting on the floor waiting to go to the laundromat. You just want to know that the house is safe and nothing is leaking or in need of repair. Tell them specifically what you are checking for.

Disclose environmental hazards such as lead.   Landlords are increasingly being held liable for tenant health problems resulting from exposure to environmental poisons in a rental property. If your rental house has lead based paint, or if your house was built before

1978, you must give them the flyer or pamphlet on lead based paints. Obviously, you would expect that your rental property has been repainted since 1978 and is covered up with nonlead based paint. Regardless, you must notify your tenants if your house was built before 1978, and make sure they are watching that the children are not chewing on the baseboards. Amazing, isn't it? How do you think the EPA discovered this was a problem? Exactly. Some kid was chewing on a window ledge or flakes of paint.

Choose and supervise your manager carefully. If a property manager commits a crime, or is incompetent, you may be held financially responsible. You must do a thorough background check and clearly spell out the manager's duties to prevent problems down the road. If you are going to use a property manager, you need to have adequate insurance on the manager, liability insurance, possibly an umbrella policy according to your agent's advice. I have chosen to do my own property management on my first house. Hopefully, my needs for a property manager will increase as my real estate portfolio expands beyond several houses.

Try to resolve disputes with tenants without lawyers and lawsuits. If you have a conflict with a tenant over rent, repairs, access to the rental unit, or some other issue that does not immediately warrant an eviction, meet with the tenant to see if the problem can be resolved informally. If that does not work, consider mediation by a neutral third party, often available at no cost from a publicly funded program. Contact your city hall for further information. If your dispute concerns money, and all attempts to reach agreement fail, try small claims court where you can represent yourself. Use it to collect unpaid rent or to seek money for property damage after a tenant moves out and the deposit is exhausted. Small claims court does not handle evicting your tenants for nonpayment. When you go to the courthouse in your state, check to see which department handles evictions and how that process is handled.

We cover evictions in Chapter 15. Here are additional reference materials available at www.nolo.com that I recommend:

- *Every Landlord's Legal Guide* by Attorney Janet Portman, Marcia Stewart, and Attorney Ralph Warner. It is $38.00 and covers the rental legalities every landlord needs to know including tenants' selections, security deposits, writing leases and rental agreements, repairs and maintenance, and much more.
- *How to Mediate Your Dispute: Find a Solution Quickly & Cheaply Outside the Courtroom* by Peter Lovenheim. It is $13.27 and shows you how to succeed using a quick, fair, and inexpensive alternative to courtroom battles. It explains each of seven mediation steps in detail. It also covers lease and rental agreement frequently asked questions.

Study leases and rental agreements. I cover leases and rental agreements in more detail in Chapter 14 but here are some quick tips while we are on the subject. The lease or rental agreement is the key document of the tenancy to set out important issues such as:

- The length of the tenancy.
- The amount of rent and deposit the tenant must pay.
- The number of people who can live on the rental property.
- Who pays the utilities.
- Whether the tenant may have pets, and if so, if it changes the deposit or other agreement terms.
- Whether the tenant may sublet the properties.
- The landlord's access to the rental property.
- Who pays attorney fees if there is a lawsuit.

You need to be as specific as possible so there is no misinterpretation of what was meant. It will be very clear and spelled out in detail. Leases and rental agreements should always be in writing, even though most states allow them to be oral or spoken. While oral agreements seem easy and informal, they often lead to disputes. If a tenant and landlord later disagree about key agreements, such as whether the tenant may sublet (rent the house out to someone else), the end result is likely to be a court argument over who said what to whom, when, and in what context.

The biggest difference between rental agreements and leases is the period of occupancy. A rental agreement provides for tenancy of a short period, often 30 days. The tenancy is automatically renewed at the end of this period, unless the tenant or landlord ends it by giving written notice, typically 30 days. For these month-to-month rentals, the landlord can change the terms of the agreement with proper written notice, subject to any rent control laws. This notice is usually 30 days, but can be shorter in some states if the rent is paid weekly or biweekly, or if the landlord and tenant have an agreement. On the other hand, a written lease gives the tenant the right to occupy the unit for a set term, most often for six months or one year and sometimes longer if the tenant pays the rent and complies with other provisions.

Unlike a rental agreement, when a lease expires it is not automatically renewed. A tenant who stays on with the landlord's consent is generally considered a month-to-month tenant. In addition, with a fixed term lease, the landlord cannot raise the rent or change other terms of the tenancy unless the changes are specifically provided for in the lease, or the tenant agrees. The lease is beneficial to the tenant because it offers fixed rent for one year, and it is beneficial to you, the landlord, because it gives you a one-year tenant, or the full deposit. Once the lease expires and the tenant goes month-to-month, you can increase the rent to market rates. For example, let us say the rent is currently $1,000 a month. The tenant stays a year and the going rate for the area is now $1,100 a month. You should increase the rent. If the tenant wants to sign another one-year lease, you may want to give them a discount rate of $1,050 for committing to another year. It is in your best interest to keep the same tenant. But balance the cost of finding a new tenant to the loss of income to keep the sure thing. Anyone who has rented knows there may be an adjustment in his or her monthly rent after the lease expires. You will want to convey this in writing at least 30 days before the increase in rent. That is when you offer a new lease.

Terms of breaking a lease. As a general rule a tenant may not legally break a lease unless the landlord significantly violates its terms. For example, if the landlord fails to make necessary repairs or fails to comply with a law concerning health or safety, the tenant may break a lease. A few states have laws that allow tenants to break leases because of health problems or job relocation that requires a permanent move. A tenant who breaks a lease without due cause will be responsible for the remainder of the rent due under the lease terms. In most states the landlord has a legal duty to try to find a new tenant as soon as possible. In other words, you cannot let the property sit empty expecting the tenant to pay. You must at least show you attempted to rent the property. You need to run an ad in the paper and put a sign in the yard. After you have rented the property again, and have an amount of loss, then you can sue for that amount in court.

A landlord may legally break the lease when a tenant significantly violates its terms of the law, for example, paying the rent late, keeping a dog in violation of a no-pets clause, substantially damaging the property, or participating in illegal activities on or near the premises, such as selling drugs. The landlord must first send the tenant the notice stating that the tenancy has been terminated. State laws set out very detailed requirements as to how a landlord must write and deliver a termination notice. Check your state laws and local attorneys.

Do not discriminate. The federal Fair Housing Act and Fair Housing Amendments Act prohibit landlords from choosing tenants on the basis of group characteristics such as:

- Race.
- Religion.
- Ethnic background or national origin.
- Gender.
- Age.
- The fact that the prospective tenant has children.
- A mental or physical disability.

In addition, some state and local laws prohibit discrimination based on a person's marital status or sexual orientation. On the other hand, landlords are allowed to select tenants using criteria based on valid business reasons such as requiring minimum income or positive references from previous landlords, as long as these standards are applied equally to all tenants.

The Fair Housing Act and Amendments prohibits landlords from taking any of the following actions based on race, religion, or any other protected category:

- Advertising, or making any statement that indicates a preference based on group characteristics such as skin color or religion.
- Falsely denying that a rental unit is available.
- Setting more restrictive standards such as higher income for certain tenants.
- Refusing to rent to members of certain groups.
- Refusing to accommodate the needs of disabled tenants such as allowing a guide dog, hearing dog, or service dog.
- Setting different terms for some tenants such as adopting an inconsistent policy of responding to late rent payments.
- Terminating a tenant for discriminatory reasons.

Know your laws. By custom, leases and rental agreements usually require the rent to be paid monthly in advance. Typically, rent is due on the first day of the month; however, it is legal for a land-lord to require rent to be paid at different intervals, or on a different day of the month. Unless the lease or rental agreement specifies otherwise, there is no legally recognized grace period. In other words, if the tenant has not paid the rent on time, the landlord can usually terminate the tenancy the day after it is due. Some landlords charge fees for late payment of rent or for bounced checks. These fees are usually legal if they are reasonable. The laws for late fees can be found in your state landlord tenant statutes.

Security deposits.   All states allow landlords to collect a security deposit when the tenant moves in. The general purpose is to assure that the tenant pays rent when due and keeps the rental unit in good condition. Half the states limit the amount landlords can charge. This is usually not more than one or two months' rent. The exact amount depends on the state. Many states require landlords to put deposits into a separate account, and some require landlords to pay tenants interest on the deposit. In the state of Georgia, if you have more than 10 rental units, you are required to have a separate account to hold deposits. If you have less than 10 units, you can commingle the deposit money with your rent money.

What are the rules for returning security deposits? The rules vary from state to state but landlords usually have a set amount of time in which to return deposits. This is usually 14 to 30 days after the tenant vacates the unit, either voluntarily or by eviction. Landlords may normally make certain deductions from the security deposit, provided they do it correctly and for an allowable reason. Many states require landlords to provide a written, itemized accounting of deductions for unpaid rent and for repairs for damages that go beyond normal wear and tear, to be sent with payment if any, of the remaining deposit balance. The rules for the keeping and/or returning of security deposits can be found in your state's landlord–tenant's statutes.

Liabilities.   In order to hold the landlord responsible, the tenant must prove that the landlord was negligent, and that the landlord's negligence caused an injury. To do this the tenant must show that:

- The landlord had control of the problem that caused the injury.
- The accident was foreseeable.
- The landlord did not give adequate warnings that would not have been unreasonably expensive or difficult.
- A serious injury was the probable consequence of not fixing the problem.
- The landlord failed to take responsible steps to avert the accident.
- The landlord's failure and negligence caused the tenant's accident.
- The tenant was genuinely injured.

For instance, if the tenant falls and breaks his ankle on a broken front doorstep, the landlord will be liable if the tenant can show that:

- It was the landlord's responsibility to maintain the steps. This would be in the lease.
- An accident of this type was foreseeable. Was it an obvious hazard to everyone?
- A repair would have been easy or inexpensive. The tenant must prove the doorstep could have been repaired with common supplies by average labor.
- The probable result of a broken step is a serious injury. What could happen and has happened in the past?

- The landlord failed to take reasonable action to maintain the steps. The landlord knew of the problem and still took no action.
- The broken step caused the injury. This will probably be assumed if not proved otherwise.
- The tenant is really hurt. In the case of a broken bone this is easy to establish.

A tenant can file a personal injury lawsuit for medical bills, lost earnings, pain, and other suffering. A tenant can also sue for property damage that results from faulty maintenance or unsafe conditions. Read your insurance policy to make sure you are covered.

Minimize financial losses and legal problems. Landlords who maintain housing in excellent condition can avoid many problems. Here's how:

- Clearly set out responsibilities for repair and maintenance in the lease or rental agreement.
- Use a written checklist to inspect the premises and fix any problems before new tenants move in.
- Encourage tenants to immediately report plumbing, heating, weatherproofing, or other defects or safety or security problems.
- Keep a written log of all tenant complaints and repair requests with details as to how and when problems were fixed. If repaired by other than the landlord, keep the invoice or get a receipt for documentation.
- Handle urgent repairs as quickly as possible taking care of major inconveniences such as plumbing or heating problems within 24 hours. Have a contingency plan if you are going to be out of reach. I use my cell phone. Therefore, if I

am out of town I can still be reached. I suggest you take phone numbers with you on vacation, or whenever you are out of the office. You want to get the issue addressed as soon as possible.

■ Twice a year give tenants a checklist on which to report potential safety hazards or maintenance problems that might have been overlooked. Use the same checklist to inspect all rental units once a year.

Here's an additional reference: *Leases and Rental Agreements* by Marcia Stewart, Attorney Ralph Warner, and Attorney Janet Portman, third edition published in January 2002; 206 pages, which include nine forms; $20.99; available at www.nolo.com.

Accounting and Rental Houses

I encourage you to set an initial appointment with two or three accountants so you can go meet them and see how your personalities are going to mesh. You also want to find a CPA who gets along with your attorney. If they have some kind of working relationship, that will be beneficial for you. You need to find someone who specializes in real estate. When you are working with your accountant, one of the first things you will need to do is set up some type of corporation. You will need to decide if you are going to buy and hold houses, or if you are going to buy and sell houses. This will determine what type of corporation you need. An LLC is a limited liability corporation. I have been advised that this is the best when you expect to buy and hold the house in order to rent it out. An S Corporation is best used when you plan to buy and sell houses. These can also be referred to as dealer and nondealer houses. A dealer house is where you plan to buy it, fix it up, and sell it. In the real estate industry it is known as flipping a house, and that is best for the S Corporation. A nondealer house is when you plan to buy it, hold it, and rent it out. That is when it is considered best to have an LLC. You can expect to pay a lawyer between $350 and $800 to form your corporation and I suggest you talk with your lawyer and accountant about what is best for you. You can expect to pay a CPA between $500 and $750 dollars per year to prepare your tax returns, and it can go up from there depending on how complicated and how many different properties, and/or different businesses or entities that you have. That is a good ballpark estimate to get you started. You might want to consider, after you have bought a couple of houses, to get a software program called QuickBooks to keep track of all of your expenses.

One of the things your accountant will want you to do is to detail your expenses. Here is a listing of them.

- Advertising.
- Auto mileage.
- Travel expenses.
- Cleaning and maintenance.
- Commissions.
- Insurance.
- Legal and other professional fees.
- Management fees.
- Mortgage interest paid to banks.
- Other interest.
- Repairs.
- Supplies.
- Taxes.
- Utilities.
- Postage.
- Business telephone, if applicable.

Use this as a minimum of listing expenses. You will have expenses that may not fit on this list. That is okay. Your accountant will work it out. You will need to keep receipts for each expense. He is going to calculate only your taxes based on the numbers that you give him. You are not going to give him the receipts. Break down these expenses per category for your CPA and just give him the numbers, but give him only the numbers for the expenses for which you have receipts. If you want to have someone sort your receipts and log them for you, then you need a bookkeeper.

Business Cards

If you have a good printer, you can make your own. Your local office supply store will have sheets of blank business cards. Using a word processing program, you can find directions for making business cards under the Help tab. I found a great web site to order colored business cards—www.vistaprint.com. If you let them put their one-line promo on the back, they charge you only for shipping. I ordered 250 colored business cards for about $9.00. I think 250 cards should last me about 10 years! You can log on to my web site at www.firstrentalhouse.com for a link to their site.

MOTIVATIONAL QUOTES

Nothing in life is to be feared. It is only to be understood.

Madam Curie

People can alter their lives by altering their attitudes.

William James

CHAPTER 8

Show Me the Money!

WHERE THE MONEY CAME FROM TO BUY MY FIRST RENTAL HOUSE

It is one thing to say "Use other people's money!" but how do you really go about doing it? This is where all the mystery seems to fog the minds of first time buyers. There are probably 100 different ways to buy a house—this is not the *best* way—this is just how I did my first deal. It seemed like the best deal for me at the time. I do not know that I will do all my future deals this way. In baseball terms, it was not a home run but it was clearly a stand-up double! The purpose of this chapter is to show you how I went about leveraging other people's money to acquire my first rental house, to give you insight as to how the process may work for you.

Just as we talked about in Chapter 3, you should take great care in finding the best loan broker you can find. My loan broker, Jill Cremens, works at The Community Bank in Loganville, Georgia, where she has access to the bank's internal lending capabilities, as well as brokering traditional 30-year mortgages outside the bank with major wholesalers. She can shop my loans from inside and outside the bank for the best possible loans. Some of the community banks have terms and types of loans that the traditional mortgage broker will not have. (See Chapter 2 for tips on finding the right loan broker for you.) It is important when you are meeting about equity lines that you have all parties who signed the original loan at the meeting. If your cousin from Texas signed and you now live in New York, you will need to get some type of power of attorney for your cousin. It is best to check with the loan officer as to what needs to be done.

The purpose of my first meeting with Jill was to accomplish two things:

1. Get my preapproval letter so that I could go see a buyer's realtor and let him/her know that I was qualified to buy a rental house. This letter would give me leverage in negotiation to show I was a serious buyer. The selling realtor listing the house will take an offer more seriously when they know the prospect can buy the house. What does that mean to you? If you were selling your house, wouldn't you be more willing to negotiate if you knew they had the money?

2. Acquire an equity line of credit on my current home to use as working capital. So at this meeting Jill knew she had one loan for the line of credit and was 99 percent certain of a loan on a second property. How responsive will she be to me in the future? Well, having two loans helps. There will be a better chance of her remembering my name when I call back.

To maximize the meeting, I brought the following documentation to the lender:

■ Two years' tax returns.
■ Three months' bank statements.

- Two months' pay stubs.
- Three months of my brokerage accounts including my IRA statements.
- Your lender will likely ask for other documentation based on your situation and the type of loan you are applying for.

These documents are routinely required for a fully documented mortgage loan. Mortgage lenders are usually buried in paperwork so if you can bring all yours in one trip, you will make a favorable impression. You also have a better chance of your documentation all getting into the correct file. As long as there are people, there are going to be mistakes. You can help yourself by being organized.

Here's how everything shook out.

Loan #1: Get Equity Line from Existing Home for Working Capital, Down Payment, and Repairs (15-Year Interest-Only at 4.75 Percent APR)

I landed the equity line of credit from my existing home to give me some working capital. When I bought our home (for our personal residence) one year ago I put 10 percent down, I got 10 percent of the purchase price in an equity line of credit, and I got 80 percent of the purchase price in a first mortgage. This is called a "combination loan" (see appendix) or some places call it a "piggyback loan" and it is designed to avoid paying private mortgage insurance. The equity line of credit that I got on my house was at prime rate, which fluctuates, and was at 4.75 percent. There was a $150 application fee and no closing costs as long as I kept the equity line of credit open for three years. Once I got the equity line of credit on my home, I had working capital to fix up the rental house. I highly recommend an equity line with one caveat. This should be used only for your primary residence or temporary funds for rental property. If you use your equity line for a Philips 42" high definition wide-screen television with six-speaker surround sound (can you tell I want one?), you have diminished the available credit on your equity line. You have also spent money on things that go down in value rather than on investments that go up. You had better enjoy that football game on that new television. It could cause you to miss a great opportunity because you did not have the cash available! And remember, the equity line is leveraged on your primary residence. If you cannot make the equity line of credit payment on the Philips 42″ high definition wide-screen television with six-speaker surround sound, you will not lose the television. You will lose the house!

Loan #2: Acquire Rental House
(Three-Year Balloon at 7 Percent APR)

When I bought the rental house, the bank was able to do a loan for 80 percent of the appraised value. We talk a lot about LTV, the abbreviation for Loan to Value. Think about it this way. If I were to buy a house appraised at $100,000 and got an 80 percent LTV, that would be an $80,000 loan. It is very important to understand that loan programs and interest rates on most types of mortgage loans are tied directly to the Loan to Value and your credit score. Sometimes the lower the risk, the better the rate. In other words, the better your credit score, the lower the risk and the lower the rate. The same goes with LTV. The lower the risk (via lower LTV), the easier to obtain the loan. If you are getting an equity line of credit and your maximum Loan to Value is only 70 percent, that is less risk to the lender than if you were to get 100 percent of the value of your house in an equity line of credit. Let us look at it this way. Your brother-in-law, whom you refer to in private as Bob the Bum, is out of work again. He needs $150 for his electric bill. (After all, he has been sitting around with the air-conditioning running full blast for a month while he was doing nothing.) The bill could be that high if not much higher! Naturally, he comes to his favorite in-law for the much needed cash. How are you feeling about this? Are you feeling the knots in your stomach? Do you see the money flying from your wallet, never to be seen again? Not a great situation is it? Now what can Bob the Bum do to lessen these emotions? Let us say he offers to loan you *his* Philips 42″ HDTV wide screen with surround sound (I am obsessed) until he pays back all the money. Now you have some collateral and a pretty low Loan to Value (LTV). You are feeling much better about this loan. You may even start looking around for another toy of Bob's he can leverage for another loan. That radial arm saw is not doing him much good right now is it?

Back to reality. The house appraised for $122,000 and needed about $5,000 to $10,000 in repairs. I offered $98,000, they countered at $101,000 and I accepted. The mortgage from the bank was for $96,700, 80 percent of $122,000. I had to put $4,300 as a down payment. (For you visual learners, see Worksheet 8.1.) I got that money from the equity line on my house (Loan #1). The purchase money I got from the bank was on a three-year balloon loan, which means I had to make payments for thirty-four months and then the entire loan amount was due on the thirty-fifth month. In the state of Georgia there is a tax at the closing that is paid on any mortgage longer than 36 months. The bank specifically wrote it for 34 months to avoid an extra fee.

The bank made the loan only because they had also found permanent financing of a 30-year mortgage (Loan #4). They knew that I would refinance that loan away from the bank. They were not going to have the loan for the entire three years, and I knew that I could not pay it off in the thirty-fifth month. I actually was qualified for two loans—one was to buy the house and another was to refinance the house on a 30-year mortgage. You may find some banks that will do this all in one loan—I have since found one in my area (New South Federal Savings Bank; 770-908-1800 or on the Web at www.newsouthfederal.com)—but have not talked to any of their customers. I encourage you to call your local banks, look in your local newspapers or magazines, and talk to other investors to see whom they are using and what type of loan programs are out there. You will be amazed at the differences from bank to bank and broker to broker. There are as many types of loans as there are flavors of ice cream.

Personally, I bank at a small community bank. Somewhere in the cobwebs of my feeble mind, I remember advice from a financial guru of some type about banking. They recommended going into the bank to conduct business whenever it was convenient. Therefore, when I need cash, I go inside instead of using the ATM. I try to make eye contact with the branch manager or the loan officer, preferably someone with an office. Why? I want them to recognize me as a customer. I might need them for business in the future. This advice will not repair your credit history. If you have a credit problem, it will not matter how familiar they are with you. However, it does show bank loyalty. After all, they have seen you in the bank so many times! Bankers like to do business with people they know.

The small community banks will be more flexible in working deals, again assuming your credit is in order. Develop that relationship. Let us face it; I would be way down the importance totem pole at Megabank. Do not get me wrong, I know I am way down that pole at the community bank, too; it is just a much shorter pole.

When we went to the closing table to buy the rental house, the sales price was $101,000, the bank gave me a loan for $96,700 and the difference in the down payment came from my current home's equity line of credit (Loan #1). In other words, *I used other people's money.*

WORKSHEET 8.1   Loan #2

Appraised value of property: $122,000

Purchase price	$101,000.00
Loan amount (appraised value * %LTV) or $122,000 * 0.80	$ 96,700.00
Down payment needed	$ 4,300.00

Loan #3: Refinance Loan #2 Based on Reappraised Value (Three-Year Balloon at 7 Percent APR)

Then, we proceeded to fix up and repair the house to increase its value. We projected needing to invest approximately $5,000 to $6,000 in materials and to hire contractors to do specific skilled work such as a locksmith to re-key the doors, and an electrician to do specific work, which we cover in the next chapter. I also had to make a mortgage payment to the bank while I was doing the renovations. I used my equity line of credit on my personal home (Loan #1) to pay for all the renovations and make the mortgage payment on the rental house.

Once we had completed all the repairs, we had the house reappraised. It then appraised for $139,000. We sent the loan back to the permanent mortgage company to see if we could get an increase in the loan amount of my permanent 30-year financing. They would refinance a 90 percent loan on that house, which equals $125,000. My permanent loan is going to be for $125,000. I owed $96,700 on the loan from the bank. I had put about $6,000 in repairs into the house.

The purpose of Loan #3 was for me to get cash out of the deal, and the three-year balloon loan enabled me to do this. Where I pre-

WORKSHEET 8.2   Loan #3

Appraised value $139,000	
Loan amount ($139,000 * 0.90)	$125,000.00
Payback of Loan #2	-$ 96,700.00
Closing costs and points on Loans #2, 3, & 4	-$ 7,300.00
Cash back at closing	$ 21,000.00
Payback of Loan #1	-$ 4,300.00
Repairs	-$ 6,000.00
Soft cost	-$ 1,500.00
Tax free profit	$ 9,200.00

viously had owed $96,700, we increased that loan amount to $125,000. Even after closing costs and points, I still ended up getting a check for $21,000. I paid back my equity line of credit (Loan #1) the $4,300 for the down payment, the $6,000 in repairs, and the $1,500 in soft costs. (Calling all visuals to Worksheet 8.2.) Soft costs consists of homeowners insurance, utilities, and so on.) The best part: I kept the rest. That amounted to about $9,200 cash *income tax free* (because loans are not taxable) going to me! Four great little words we are all working for *Tax Free to Me!*

Loan #4: Get a 30-Year Fixed Rate Mortgage (at 6.625 Percent APR)

Within 15 minutes of closing on Loan #3, I signed the paperwork on Loan #4. I essentially refinanced Loan #3 into a 30-year fixed rate loan to lower my payment and make it consistent for the next 30 years (or however long I keep the property). Loan #4 would not allow cash back at the closing table. Therefore we did Loan #3 to get our cash out.

RENTAL HOUSE POINTS VERSUS PRIMARY HOUSE POINTS

When you get a permanent 30-year mortgage on a rental house, you are going to have some additional fees that you might not have on your primary home. For example, you will pay two points, or 2 percent of the loan amount, as a premium to the mortgage company for accepting higher risk on a rental house than they would have on a primary home. (The numbers work this way: 2% of $125,000 is $2,500.) The logic from the mortgage company goes like this: If, for instance, you get laid off and your money gets tight, you will quit making the rental house payments before you quit making the payments on your primary home. There is higher risk to the lender on the rental house than on a primary home. Remember Bob the Bum, you know, your brother-in-law? Miraculously he has landed a job, which requires the use of his radial arm saw, which you have since acquired. Which loan do you think he will be paying you back first? Bingo! You still have that Philips 42" high definition wide-screen television with surround sound for a little while longer.

Points on a primary house are usually "discount" points and are prepaid interest to get a lower interest rate. Most lenders do not recommend paying discount points unless the seller pays for them. In other words, if your seller will pay $4,000 in closing costs and your deal involves closing costs of only $3,000 then apply that unused money to discount points or prepaid interest. As a general rule 1 percent or 1 point will lower your rate $\frac{1}{8}$ to a $\frac{1}{4}$ of a percent. The difference in principal and interest payments on a 30-year fixed rate mortgage of $100,000 with interest rates of:

$6\frac{7}{8}\%$ (also expressed as 6.875%) is about $657 per month rounded up.

7% is about $665 per month rounded up.

$7\frac{1}{8}\%$ (also expressed as 7.125%) is about $674 per month rounded up.

PRIVATE MORTGAGE INSURANCE

Anytime you obtain a single mortgage above 80 percent Loan to Value, the lender usually requires you to pay private mortgage insurance, or PMI. (See the appendix for "combination loan.") On this house it is about $95.00 per month in private mortgage insurance. This is to protect the lender. You will find it difficult, but not impossible, to get an equity line of credit on a rental house. It is much easier to get a 90 percent mortgage on a rental house than it is to get an 80 percent first mortgage and a 10 percent equity line on a rental house. Lenders are very hesitant to lend money on an equity line on a rental house. In our case, we did a 90 percent first mortgage.

Previously, we had a primary residence reappraised at our expense in order to drop the PMI. The appraisal was $250.00. The

PMI was about $60 per month. After five months, we saw an increase in our monthly net income. Understand that rules vary; this technique may not work with all mortgage companies. In this area, houses generally appreciate at an average rate of three percent to five percent per year. Therefore, in four years, I will investigate housing values in the area and see if dropping PMI is a possibility. I could use another $95 a month. Couldn't you?

In Worksheet 8.2 you will notice a large dollar amount for closing costs. There are two reasons for this. One, there are two loans we are closing. Loans #2 and #3 are both paid in this worksheet. Two, we had to pay a two-point fee for a rental house plus we had to pay closing costs to the attorney.

THE BOTTOM LINE

I actually went to the closing table four times to buy my first rental house. But in the end I did it with none of my own money down and was able to pull $9,000 out of the house tax free! Now I could use that $9,000 to pay my own bills, or put it into a reserve account to make mortgage payments on the rental house in case I had delays in renting it (which I did). I could use it to pay for advertising in the newspapers or whatever I wanted, or I could use the $9,000 as a down payment on the next house. I put it to much better use than for that Philips 42″ high definition wide-screen TV with six-speaker surround sound. (Did I mention that it has picture-in-picture capabilities? It's so sweet.)

This is a prime example of using other people's money, and in the final analysis I had no money down and pulled $9,000 out of the house, tax free. Is this a great country or what? Remember those four fabulous little words—Tax Free to Me.

Let me summarize the steps I took:

1. Got preapproved for a rental house loan (Loan #2).
2. Obtained an equity line of credit on my current home (Loan #1).

3. Signed the sales contract on the rental house.
4. Got approved for two loans (Loan #2 and Loan #4)
5. Bought the house.
6. Fixed up the house (me back is still sore!).
7. Got new appraisal.
8. Modified or increased the purchase loan (Loan #3). This gave me cash.
9. Refinanced the modified loan from 34 months to 30 years (Loan #4).
10. Rented the house.
11. Got real good at signing our names!

CHAPTER 9

Welcome to the Closing Table!

When you arrive at the closing attorney's office, you will be led into the room where you will complete the deal. Take a look at the center of the conference table. What do you see? There should be enough pens for a large fifth grade classroom. This is a big hint of what is to come. You will get more papers shoved into your face for you to sign than you care to count. You may have writer's cramp by the time you finish. After you walk out of the closing, you will have already forgotten the purpose for each form. Later are the names of a couple of the disclosures that are required by the Real Estate Settlement Procedures Act (RESPA).

At a typical closing, you will have the following attendees:

- Purchaser: That would be you and whoever is signing for the loan with you. If your parents are signing for the loan, they need to be present or give you power of attorney.

- Purchaser's real estate agent: They are paid to assist with your closing. You should expect them to be there. However, it is not required. Generally, they are happy to be there because they get paid at closing. The managing realtor for your broker may require that they attend all closings. So if you decide you do not want them there, and they insist, it is because they have to.
- Seller: Obvious enough! The same rules apply here as with the purchaser. All parties with their names on the warranty deed, or whatever legal document your state uses, must attend or have a power of attorney to represent that individual. During the closing for the rental property there was no seller present. In our case the bank that had foreclosed the house was located in Texas so the bank did not have a representative present. However, the bank had signed the closing documents the day before and had them sent by overnight carrier to our closing.
- Seller's real estate agent: Again, obvious enough! With our foreclosure purchase, there was no real estate agent present.

You can see how the conference table can get crowded. However, this is not always the case. The closing on our current primary residence was the smallest possible group. The house was a relocation resale. Therefore, the company gave power of attorney to the closing attorney. Our realtor, tired from waiting on the six-hour "closing from hell" on the house we sold, had asked that we pick up the check for her. My wife, the attorney, and I signed all the papers in about 10 minutes. The "closing from hell," which had ended about 30 minutes before this one, had seven attendees. Even the mortgage broker had attended! That is why they have so many pens! Look for my next book *How to Avoid the Closing from Hell!!* You might want to keep the pen from the closing table as a souvenir—but do not expect it to be any nicer than a BIC stick pen.

The Real Estate Settlement Procedures Act (RESPA) is a consumer protection statute, first passed in 1974, and administered by the U.S.

Department of Housing and Urban Development's (HUD) Federal Housing Administration (FHA). The purposes of RESPA are:

- To help consumers get fair settlement services by requiring that key service costs be disclosed in advance. There were once horror stories of fees that were never mentioned until at the closing table. The buyer, who had a deposit on a moving van and a family ready to move, paid the fees just to get into the house.
- To eliminate kickbacks and referral fees that unnecessarily increase the costs of certain settlement services. This makes it easier to get the best services for your situation, not your loan officer's buddy who pays him $500 for each new referred loan.
- To protect consumers from any additional practices that would increase the cost of settlement services.

Yes, it is a good thing! However, it will seem like a few good trees gave their lives so you could be informed. RESPA requires that you, the borrower, receive disclosures at various times during the closing, or settlement process. Disclosures spell out the costs associated with the settlement; they outline lender servicing and escrow account practices and explain the business relationship among settlement service providers.

RESPA REQUIRED DISCLOSURES

At the Time of the Loan Application

When you apply for a mortgage loan, mortgage brokers and/or lenders must provide:

- *Special Information Booklet,* which contains consumer information on various real estate settlement services. This is actually produced by your lender, under the RESPA guidelines.

- *Good Faith Estimate (GFE)* of settlement costs, which lists the charges you are likely to pay at settlement. It will also let you know if the lender requires you to use a particular settlement service. This is the time for you to ask questions. If something does not look on paper like it sounded when they explained it to you, they need to do some more explaining! If they cannot explain it to your satisfaction, it is not too late to cancel the deal with this company. There are mortgage companies on every street corner. The loss of a $200–$500 application fee is worth changing companies if it saves you thousands of dollars at the closing or over the life of the loan.
- *Mortgage Servicing Disclosure Statement,* which tells you whether the lender intends to keep the loan or to transfer it to another lender for servicing, and also gives information about how you can resolve complaints, if needed. Later in this chapter there is an explanation of what will happen if the loan is transferred.

The lender has three days to mail this information if not presented at the time of application.

Before the Closing Occurs

The **HUD-1 Settlement Statement** is a standard form that clearly shows all charges incurred for borrowers and sellers in connection with the closing. A sample HUD-1 Settlement Statement is available online at www.hud.gov. RESPA allows the borrower to request to see the HUD-1 Settlement Statement one day before the actual closing. The closing agent must then provide you with a completed HUD-1 Settlement Statement based on current information. If you are working with a real estate agent, they should review the information, also. While this sounds good in a textbook, the reality is that mortgage companies and closing attorneys are so busy that they rarely get the closing package completed until the day of closing. No fear, you can always correct mistakes while sitting at the closing table. Enter the wonderful world of word processing!

Due to a variety of reasons, closing attorneys' offices are very busy the last week of the month. Expect delays, mistakes, and short tempers if you wait until the thirtieth to close. If at all possible, try to close during the first week of the month. See your mortgage broker for more details.

At Closing

You will get the HUD-1 Settlement Statement, which shows the actual settlement costs of the loan transaction. Separate forms may be prepared for you and the seller. We have gone through three HUD-1 Settlement Statements in 10 minutes during one closing. One time they even had the address wrong. So please review the statement carefully.

The **Initial Escrow Statement** itemizes the estimated taxes, insurance premiums, and other charges anticipated to be paid from the escrow account during the first 12 months of the loan. It lists the escrow payment amount and any required cushion. Although the statement is usually given at closing, the lender has 45 days from closing to deliver it. The escrow is reviewed annually for any needed adjustments in your monthly payments.

After Closing

Loan servicers must also provide you with an **Annual Escrow Statement** once a year. The annual escrow account statement summarizes all escrow account deposits and payments during the servicer's 12-month computation year. It also notifies you of any shortages or overages in the account. If needed, the loan servicer will notify you of any change in the payment because of a shortage or overage.

A Servicing Transfer Statement is required if the loan servicer sells or assigns the servicing rights to your loan to another loan servicer. Generally, the loan servicer must notify you 15 days before the effective date of the loan transfer. The notice will include the name and address of the new servicer, toll-free telephone numbers, and the date the new servicer will begin accepting payments. This is a very common practice in the mortgage world, so be prepared to see this happen at least once on your mortgage. Financially, it will not affect you at all. The only difference is you will have new mailing labels for your payment address.

CHAPTER 10

Rehabbing Your Rental House

Okay. You have bought your first rental house. Now it is time to fix it up and make it attractive to prospective renters. You might be intimidated by the tasks that lie ahead. But have no fear! You do not have to be a full-time professional developer or remodeler to successfully rehab your rental house. If someone like me, who works a full-time job and has family responsibilities, can do it over the course of a few weekends, there is hope for you! Here is the breakdown as to how I got my house ready for renters.

TAKING STOCK

Before I made an offer on my first rental house, my real estate agent Tommy and I evaluated how much renovation work would be needed. Did the carpets need to be replaced or could they be steam cleaned? How much work would the bathrooms require? How did we stand in regard to plumbing? Other costs we needed to factor in our thinking were new door locks, pressure washing the driveway, deck, and siding, and resealing the deck and all routine maintenance items, such as cleaning out the gutters. We then assessed about how long the whole rehab process would take, what work I could do myself, and what work would need an outside contractor. I was initially told that the house needed between $5,000 and $10,000 in work. The difference between $5,000 and $10,000 would be if I did it myself or not. I was going to try to do as much of the work myself and save some money. Prior to closing on the house, I contacted my church's Spanish ministry, through which I could hire temp workers to work on Saturdays for $10.00 per hour. I projected that I would need about $5,000 in materials if I did most of the labor and hired part-time labor. Log on to www.firstrental-house.com to see the before and after pictures.

THE FIRST SATURDAY

The People: *Me, tree cutter, pest control guy, locksmith.*
The Objectives: *Replace door locks, remove extraneous trees, improve curb appeal, take care of pest control, start work on master bath.*
The Time: *8 A.M. to 5 P.M.*
Materials/Contractors: *5 gallons of Kilz primer, Wagner paint roller, drop cloths, brushes, rollers, 100-foot roll of plastic about 8 feet wide, replacement shower, 6 bales of pine straw, locksmith, North American Tree Service, miscellaneous hardware and tools, pressure washing supplies, chain and locks for the borrowed trailer.*
The Cost: *$1,063.*

I must have miscommunicated with the translator at church because no one showed up to help me that Saturday. There I waited at the church, bright and early, with a bag of chicken biscuits in hand, optimism in my heart, and a borrowed utility trailer full of tools hooked up to the back of my van. When I called the correspondent for the Spanish ministry, no one was there and all I got was the answering machine. I was now a *real* landlord—lots of work and problems—and on my own! *What Was I Thinking*! I went on to the house without any helpers—frustrated and pessimistic about the amount of work ahead of me.

The first thing I did was to hire a locksmith to re-key the doors for security reasons. I also ordered the largest trash dumpster (30 cubic yards) delivered to the driveway. On that first day the tree service showed up and cut down the tree in the back and laid it in the yard. We also cut down the overgrown landscaping that had grown up along the other side of the house. I had weeds growing five feet tall along the side of the house and overgrown bushes by the front window. I cut everything back and then pressure washed the outside of the house. This house has aluminum siding, and pressure washing really cleaned it up and put it back in like-new condition. Just cutting down all the overgrown landscaping and pressure washing the outside of the house made a huge improvement in the curb appeal of the home. I also pressure washed the deck to prepare it for sealing at a later time. I had a pest control man come out and initially treat the house for bugs, as I need to keep cockroaches and ants to a minimum.

This first weekend I laid down some plastic sheeting in the master bedroom and proceeded to remove the shower walls out of the master bath and lay them onto the plastic protected carpet. The bath had a tile shower, the tile had not been properly maintained over the years, and even some of the tiles in the shower were literally falling off. The shower head had leaked and had ruined the drywall around it. I took a small, handheld drywall saw that is about six inches long and cut along the tile around the master bath shower. The floor (also known as a "pan") was made of fiberglass. I left that in place. If it had been a tile floor, I would have had to rip that up as well. I just needed to scrub the fiberglass pan at a later time. As I cut out the shower tile, I took out it and the drywall together, cutting it back to the studs. I then pulled out these pieces and set them on the plastic inside the master bedroom to have the workers take out to the dumpster at a later time. I did the fun part and would let them do the cleanup part! Once I had ripped out the master bath down to the studs, I could replace that with green drywall. There is a special drywall that goes in wet areas like bathrooms and kitchens. It looks like drywall but has a green face on it. It is more moisture resistant than regular drywall. On subsequent weekends I was able to replace that drywall and put in a new five-piece fiberglass shower surround that I had bought at Home Depot for about $120.00. That first weekend all I really did was cut out the shower and have some of the subcontractors (utilities, locksmith, tree service, and dumpster) come in.

THE SECOND SATURDAY

The People: *Me, workers from church, electrician/plumber.*
The Objectives: *Cut lawn, fix plumbing and wiring, seal deck.*
The Time: *8 A.M. to 5 P.M.*
Materials/Contractors: *Electrician/plumber, more paint and supplies, saw blades and nails, and a new stove at the scratch and dent store. Plus—a huge dumpster rented from Waste Management.*
The Cost: *$1,031.*

I was back in communication with the Spanish ministry of my church and got my workers lined up. I was concerned with how I could communicate with them if they did not speak enough English. I have a good friend who is bilingual. I took her to lunch on Friday. I have a small digital voice recorder that I use on my way to work and commuting around town to record messages of things to do. I have carried this digital voice recorder with me for a year. What I was able to do was write down 20 different sentences or orders that I thought I would want these workers to do. I wrote them down on a sheet of paper and numbered them 1 through 20. Back to my friend at lunch: I said the sentence or order in English and my friend repeated it in Spanish. The digital voice recorder has a liquid crystal display that counts each time you record a message. I recorded number 1 and that matched the number 1 on my sheet of paper, so if I asked the number 10 item, it matched the number 10 item on my sheet. If I needed to jump from number 1 to number 16, the workers knew exactly which item I was having them do. I had things like "Please throw this into the trash." "Please plant these bushes right where I have placed them." "My wife and children will bring us lunch today." With the variety of items that I had recorded in English and Spanish, if we had any problems with communication, I could resort to my digital voice recorder. I had paid about $70.00 for the Olympus digital voice recorder at Circuit City. It was like having my own translator at the job site.

The second weekend the workers showed up. I had some fresh biscuits for them. I played the digital voice recorder to let them know what we were going to do. Their eyes lit up at what this little magic box said. We cleaned up all the landscaping debris in the yard including the tree that had been cut down, the bushes, and the weeds that I had cut down. We cleaned up the outside of the house and cut the grass to give it some curb appeal. People could see that this house was being renovated. This also cut down on possible vandalism by letting people know there was now someone in the house.

After we had cleaned up the outside of the house, we cleaned the trash out of the crawl space. The old gas oven was so nasty and filthy that we decided to throw it away rather than try to clean it. We bought a new gas oven at a scratch and dent place for $180.00.

This weekend we filled the dumpster. My wife could not believe first that I had gotten such a big dumpster, and second that we had filled it up with trash from the current house.

I had an electrician/plumber come in and do a little bit of electrical work. I wanted to be sure it was done to building code so if I ever decided to sell the house, it would be up to code. Some wires in the attic looked like they had been cut improperly. I had him repair that area and also some plumbing work under the kitchen sink. The previous owners had some strange water filter system in the house that looked like it had not been properly maintained or cleaned and like it would make the water dirtier instead of cleaner. I had him remove this complex looking filter system and make sure it all worked properly.

We put a sealer on the deck during this weekend. I do not like to use Thompson's water sealer because it is too watery and does not last very long. I was told by a professional painter friend of mine to use an oil based stain. You probably will not be able to buy oil based stains much longer because of the environmental issues, but even a clear oil based stain is going to last much longer than Thompson's water sealer. We also cleaned out all the gutters. We had a full weekend of work.

THE THIRD SATURDAY

The People: *Me, workers from church.*
The Objectives: *Repair deck supports, renovate bathrooms, continue to improve curb appeal.*
The Time: *8A.M. to 5 P.M.*
Materials/Contractors: *Duplicate keys and tags for the front door, wood screws for the deck, white paint, beige paint, supplies, and 18 bales of pine straw.*
The Cost: *$192.*

Some cement blocks that the former owners had used on the front of the house as a border for some landscaping did not look very good. We removed all those and brought them around to the back of the house and secured the deck. It had a couple of metal poles holding up the end, and they were rusted and beginning to rot out.

We propped up the deck on some concrete blocks, and we literally jacked up the deck with a car jack enough so that we could get in there and secure it with concrete blocks. We used a level to make sure that the deck leaned away from the house slightly so that if it rained, the water would tend to run away from the house. We leveled it from side to side and secured the deck. We also made the mistake of starting to paint with primer on the third weekend. We say we made the mistake because we should have continued to do all the destruction before we started the construction. We took out the master bathroom cabinet, which meant we had to take out the sink. We kept the sink and put it back in later. We also ripped out the two layers of linoleum flooring in the master bath (some groovy lime green stuff underneath!). We installed a new oven; I pressure washed the driveway; we installed some new bushes around the front of the house, and we also painted the front door trim to give it some more curb appeal. We installed a new light fixture so it was a bright, shiny fixture rather than an old pitted, rusty fixture on the front door. This cleaned up the curb appeal of the front entryway.

THE FOURTH SATURDAY

The People: *Me, Nan, worker from church.*

The Objectives: *Repair ceiling, install new tile in master bath, renovate hall bathroom.*

The Time: *8:30 A.M. to 6 P.M.*

Materials/Contractors: *Pest control, paint brushes, hand tools, chimney cap, bath and towel bars, drywall, door/knobs, tub surround, drywall supplies, bathroom cabinet.*

The Cost: *$744.*

We cut the grass again. A couple of holes in the ceiling needed to be patched and repaired. One of them looked like someone had been walking around up in the attic and had put their foot through the ceiling. The house previously had a leak in the ceiling in the living room before the owners had replaced the roof a couple of years ago, and there was a wet, or a soft spot, in one part of the ceiling. As people had come through and looked at the house, they would all poke their fingers into this soft spot in the ceiling. From the time I looked at the house until the time I closed and got in, enough people had put their fingers into this hole that this part had to be replaced as well.

We installed the master bathroom backer board to the floor in order to install the new tile. We also installed the five-piece shower surround in the master bathroom, and then we started to work on the hallway bath. It had a pink tile surround on the tub. The tile was in good shape, but the grout in between the tile had been caulked (rather than re-grouted) and had gotten full of mildew and looked terrible. My wife had spent a couple of hours one day trying to clean up the grout in the tile, and we ended up deciding we would just rip out the pink surround.

On the fourth weekend we had a new dumpster, a smaller one this time, and we went ahead and ripped out the hall bath tile surround. It had a tub and a shower so we kept the fiberglass tub, but for the tile surround we used the handsaw for drywall to cut right around the edge of it and pulled that out down to the studs. We also replaced the sliding glass doors on the master shower. Log on to www.firstrentalhouse.com to see the pictures.

THE FIFTH SATURDAY

The People: *Me, worker from church.*
The Objectives: *Finish hall bathroom, paint interior.*
The Time: *8 A.M. to 6:30 P.M.*
Materials/Contractors: *Mortgage payment, paint, cleaning supplies, contact paper.*
The Cost: *$1,008.*

On the fifth weekend, we installed the hall bath shower surround, which included new drywall and a five-piece fiberglass surround kit that you buy at Home Depot that is designed strictly for remodeling. It cost about $120.00.

We painted and painted and painted that fifth weekend. We painted with primer. We painted the hallways and the bedrooms. We even painted the bedroom ceilings with white primer. We were using a brand called Kilz, because we have had better luck with that brand of primer. We had purple bedroom walls and pink bedroom walls that we had to cover with primer. We put up two coats of primer before we started to finish coat the walls.

We also decided to paint the dark kitchen cabinets white. We painted them with two coats of primer as well. We did a lot of painting that weekend.

We also grouted the master bath tile.

THE SIXTH SATURDAY

The People: *Me, worker from church.*
The Objectives: *Finish painting interior, repair basement door.*
The Time: *9 A.M. to 5 P.M.*
Materials/Contractors: *Kitchen and hall bath trim, plumbing supplies.*
The Cost: *$222.*

On the sixth weekend we painted and painted. After we had primed the walls, we painted with beige colored paint. We painted all the walls beige except the kitchen and the baths, which we painted white. We bought premixed paint. In other words, we did not have to stand in line during the weekend and have them try to match a color. We bought a premixed paint off the shelf so that I can go in to any Lowe's and buy that very same color. What I got off the bottom label of the can was the color number. I cut off the label and put it into my wallet so I made sure that I could match that color if I had to go to a different Lowe's and buy another gallon of paint.

We also installed quarter round trim down on the floor in the kitchen and in the hall bath because when they had put down new linoleum they had not done a very good job, and they had taken it right up to the trim rather than pull the trim off the walls, put down the new linoleum, and put the new trim on top. Some of the linoleum was starting to curl up around the trim. What I did was put down quarter round on top of it and that pushed all the linoleum down and gave it a more finished look.

We also replaced the sliding glass doors in the basement. The seal had become cracked, or was not sealing any more, and the two panes of glass had allowed moisture to go in between the two panes of glass, and it had fogged up those sliding glass doors to the point where you could not see out. I had those replaced by a contractor.

There was a broken window on the front of the house. I had the same contractors do that, but I will get to the nightmare of getting that front window replaced a little later. They had to take measurements twice, and have the window made three times before they got it right. It took over a month to replace one window.

THE SEVENTH SATURDAY

The People: *Me, carpet cleaner, window repair guy.*
The Objectives: *Install new door knobs, replace broken front window, cut grass, steam clean carpets and air ducts.*
The Time: *10 A.M. to 4 P.M.*
Materials/Contractors: *Electrical outlets and supplies, carpet and duct cleaning, light switch and outlet wall plates, for rent sign, paid the Visa bill for the shower doors, tile, and supplies.*
The Cost: *$918.*

On the seventh weekend we installed all new doorknobs on the freshly painted doors, so that all the doorknobs inside matched and had a fresh shine. I got doorknobs for $6.00 to $7.00 each. We cut the grass again. They finally replaced the broken front window. I steam cleaned the carpet and the central air-conditioning ducts.

This is a story I have to tell: I received a full-page, full-color flyer in my home for a carpet cleaning service. I called and scheduled a time to meet them at the house. They are supposed to be there at 9 A.M. but by 9:30 A.M. they have not arrived. I call them to see what has happened. Well, they did not have me on the schedule—they had put it on their schedule on the wrong day. Here I am—I have taken time off work to meet someone out there and they have not shown up. Now I am frustrated—they are supposed to be cleaning my carpets and I am getting *nothing* accomplished. I want to get the house on the market to rent. I need the carpets cleaned and the air-conditioning vents vacuumed. I am venting some of my frustrations on this carpet cleaning company and asking them why they would place a full-page ad in a flyer and send it to my house and then not have people who can accurately record what day to come out and do the job. In the process of just venting some of my frustrations, they did not know how to handle a frustrated customer. They actually *cussed* me out on the phone! I am shocked. I call back and tell the secretary to please tell the manager that I was just cussed out by the man who schedules appointments.

She said *he is* the manager; she is shocked as well. I decided I am not going to do business with them (tough decision!).

Here I am, sitting at the house, deciding what I am going to do. I have just received a yellow pages book the weekend before. I open the yellow pages and try to find a carpet cleaning company close to the rental house that has a good sized ad. The first one I call is not able to come out for at least a week. I then call the one with largest ad in the yellow pages. They answer and have a man on his way toward the house. He has one job to do and will be at my house after lunch and can do it today.

It turns out he is a supernice professional man. He is able to steam clean all the carpets that day and clean out all the air ducts and really clean the house. After he was finished I put new register covers down on top of the heating and air ducts to have them look new and shiny and clean.

It was interesting, in dealing with some of these different contractors how I was treated by them.

MONDAY MORNING QUARTERBACK

Keep in mind, when I went about renovating my first rental house, I was not an expert at it. I read books, talked with experienced people, and kind of stumbled my way through it, learning on the job. So what I am going to do here is critique how I did. What did I do right? What would I have done differently? By learning from my experience, you can save time, money, and effort when you rehab your first rental house.

What Did I Do Right?

The first thing was finding the biggest dumpster that Waste Management could bring into the house, bigger than I ever thought I would need. As we were cleaning out, we found more and more debris to throw into the dumpster. Do get one much bigger than you would ever think you will need.

I painted all the bedroom walls and the floor trim the same color because it was faster. I had taken old manila file folders and stuck them under the trim and then had a drop cloth on the floor as well so that we could paint as quickly as possible and paint right down to the floor. We let the paint dry and pulled up the file folders and did not get any paint on the carpet—at least not in the bedrooms.

Also, painting the ceiling with primer made that job go pretty quickly because I painted the walls and ceiling in one step. I could use a roller to the top of the wall and just keep going across the top of the ceiling. It made the ceilings look bright, clean, and new.

I painted the inside of the house two colors—beige and white. The bedrooms, hallway, and living room are all beige. The bathrooms, kitchen, doors, and door trim are painted white. I used pre-mixed colors everywhere so that all rental houses I buy in the future will all be painted the same colors. If I have to do any touchup work it will all be the same colors. I learned that tip from Carlton Sheets—which I think is a super idea.

If you have to paint the outside of the house, John Adams suggests a yellow house with white trim and dark green shutters.

Another thing I thought I did right was that I was very nice to the workers who showed up. When the man came to cut down the tree on Saturday, I gave him a $10.00 cash tip for coming out on a Saturday. I had a cooler full of bottled water and Gatorade. To any contractor who came out I offered a water or Gatorade, and in just treating people as I would like to be treated, I felt I had really good service from people and was treated very well.

What Would I Do Differently the Next Time?

I will start by putting down a protective plastic layer on the flooring all through the house. Even though the floor may be dirty at the time, I am going to keep myself from getting paint and drywall mud on my shoes and then walking through the house and getting it on the carpet, which I did.

I would also do all of the construction work on the house first and do all of the painting last. I was in a hurry to start painting over those purple and pink walls. The kids' bedrooms even had markers on the walls. I should have taken more time and done all the construction work first and saved the painting for last. I would get all the construction tools out of the way before I began painting—I was tripping over containers of hand tools.

GETTING THE MOST BANG FOR YOUR RENOVATION BUCK

Three areas you really want to make sure you do well: You want to have good curb appeal by cutting the grass, cleaning up the front door, cutting back the landscaping, getting rid of the weeds, and putting down fresh pine straw. You do not need an extravagant flowerbed or extravagant landscaping, but simple landscaping and clean. If you have wood trim around the front door, be sure that it is freshly painted. Make sure any light fixture at the front door is working, the light bulb is on, and it is a clean, polished front fixture. If you can polish the one that is there, you will not have to buy a new one. I had some spotlights on the outside of the house for night use, and I made sure those spotlights were replaced and turned on, so people who drove by at night would see that the house looked very safe and inviting. You should also spend your money on kitchens and bathrooms. As my wife puts it, "Any place you are going to eat or be naked you want to look very clean."

I would not spend a lot of money on the backyard landscaping. I would never buy a house that had a swimming pool. If a house came with an above-ground pool, I would have it taken out and sell it through the newspaper. I do not want to have a rental house that has a swimming pool. There is too much liability. If the neighbor kids jump the fence and drown in your pool, some lawyer will sue you for it.

I do not want to spend a lot of money on extravagant landscaping or to have expensive drapes or lots of different colors of paint inside the house that I would have to keep on hand for touchups. If I have four different colors of paint inside the house, I have to have four different colors of paint for touchups—multiply that by seven to eight houses some day. I keep it very simple with beige and white.

Hiring Subcontractors: What to Look for, How to Avoid Getting Ripped Off, How I Found Them, and How to Stay on Top of Their Work

You could easily write a book on how to find subcontractors and how to deal with them. Referrals and word of mouth are the best sources of whom to use for subcontractors.

For dumpsters I called three or four different places. I ended up using the trash service where I could talk to a human being. They were polite and I had seen their dumpsters around town so I knew they were a large company with lots of delivery services. They could deliver one on the day I wanted, and they could pick it up on the day I stated. They did not charge me a per-day fee while it sat there. Some companies wanted to charge a per-day fee while the dumpster was there.

I also found a locksmith the same way. I called one who was close to the house, who could come when it was convenient for me, and who had a competitive price. Again, I dealt with someone who answered the phone. I do not like leaving messages for contractors. I want to deal with a person who answers the phone.

I had used my electrician and plumber for some work on my personal home. He is both a licensed electrician and a licensed plumber. I like using him because I can get two skills in one person and only have one fee for trip costs. Most plumbers will have a $75.00 fee just to show up and so will the electrician. By having a man who does both I can eliminate one of those fees. I found mine through a lead-sharing club that I was in and who had previously done work on my home.

I told you the horror story of trying to use a full-page flyer that came in my mailbox for someone who appeared reputable for carpet cleaning. When I called I got to talk to a human being, but when the day came they did not show up on time. I ended up using a small mom-and-pop service and the man I called was the man who came to clean the carpets. He had answered on his cell phone and came that day—I simply got lucky.

With all the preparations that you take you will still have some subs who will not do the work as you had hoped. Again, word of mouth referrals from people who have used those subs in the past are your best guarantee.

I had to replace sliding glass windows and I had a broken window on the front of the house. I searched the Internet for sliding glass door manufacturers and called one for a referral to work on my house. They gave me the name of a guy who answered his cell phone on the way to Florida for vacation. He promised to come do the work when he got back—but even with repeated calls he never showed up. So much for that idea on using referrals from manufacturers.

I was at a gas station getting gas in my car when a window replacement subcontractor pulled up next to me. They had replacement windows and glass on their truck. The workers who got out of the truck appeared to be the kind of men whom I wanted to have in my home. They looked clean-cut and were well spoken. I asked one of them if he had a business card on him which he did not, but he wrote down on a piece of paper whom the dispatcher was and whom to talk to for a quote. I went by their shop and it appeared to be very clean and well-run. I could talk to a person. It was not run out of someone's back garage with a cell phone and pager. They put the sliding glass doors in as described, but the front window had to be measured twice and they made the window three different times before they put it in. I was very frustrated. It took six weeks to replace one window. I will not use them again. Maybe I need to be in the replacement window business.

When you work with subcontractors, never pay them until the work is completed. Some of the worst horror stories of scams and ripoffs by subcontractors have been when they have you pay for materials or labor before starting the work. Never, never, never do this. Legitimate contractors never ask for money up front. When I had some major work done on my personal home, I would pay the subcontractor as some of the work was completed. I paid him on a draw of the work that was completed, and he paid for all of the materials. *Never pay for work until it is completed.*

When I deal with mom-and-pop contractors, I make it a habit to pay them quickly. Some of them will have me pay them as soon as the work is completed. The locksmith had me write him a check on the spot when he had completed the work. My tree service was the same way. My pest control man and my plumber/electrician sent me an invoice. The day I get their invoice, I write them a check and mail it to them. I want them to know—especially the mom-and-pops—that if I need to ask for special service, I am one who pays his bills promptly. They will respond the next time to someone who pays their bills quickly, rather than to someone who strings them along for 60 or 90 days. The quicker you pay subcontractors, the better response you will have the next time you need them. Think how you like to be treated.

MOTIVATIONAL QUOTES

Genius is one percent inspiration and ninety-nine percent perspiration.
Thomas Edison

Lazy hands make a man poor, but diligent hands bring wealth.
Proverbs 10:4

CHAPTER 11

How I Landed a Tenant

After I had rehabbed the house and it was ready to occupy, I decided to try to start with a lease/purchase rather than a rental tenant agreement. In a lease/purchase situation the person coming in and living in the house is going to have more of an ownership mentality than a rentership mentality. At the time, I thought a lease/purchase tenant would be better for us than a rental tenant. (And it still might, but things just did not work out that way in this instance.)

Here is why I started out on a lease/purchase: If somebody has marginal credit, a divorce, or a medical bankruptcy—something that indicates they need two or three years to pay off some of their outstanding loans or liens on their credit report—a lease/purchase is a viable plan for home ownership. Possibly they just went through a messy divorce and have a number of late payments, and they need to show two or three years of having consistently paid their bills on time before they can get a home mortgage. A lease/purchase is a great way for them to buy a house.

A basic lease/purchase works something like this: You must obtain a special investment house appraisal that shows what the comparable rents are in the area. In my case, it was $1,050 per month. Anything in excess of the current market rents can be applied to the down payment on the house. If they can afford an extra $100 or $200 per month, that amount would be applied to the down payment when they buy the house. If they made a monthly payment of $1,250 per month for 36 months their down payment would be $7,200 (36 months × $200). Plus, when someone comes in to a lease/purchase, they generally put down more than one month's rent for a security deposit. Instead of putting $1,000 down they might put $1,500 or $2,000 down. This is a great way for someone who has just gone through some negative financial event in their life, or someone who has trouble saving money on their own, and they need a plan to buy into a house two or three years from now.

Caution: Fannie Mae and Freddie Mac use the previous scenario as their guidelines. If you tell someone you will apply half of their monthly payment toward the down payment, they will have a tough time getting that loan approved.

I feel the reason a lease/ purchase did not work on my first rental house is that interest rates have been so low for so long that anyone who could buy a house did so. The lending programs available today are so liberal and lenient, that in some cases you do not even need a down payment on a first time home buyer mortgage. However, this trend is starting to change, as the lenient programs of today will soon be withdrawn as the foreclosure rates go up. Also, many states are enacting laws that affect the way mortgage companies do business.

MARKETING, MARKETING, MARKETING

How did I find a renter for my first rental house? Here is the process including the good, the bad, and the ugly I went through to land a good renter. Take note of lessons learned—to save you time, money, and headaches!

To start, I put a sign in the front yard that said "Lease/ Purchase, 3 bedrooms, $2^1/_2$ baths. Toll-free message." I had a toll-free 800 telephone number through a company called Pro Quest Technologies. The 800 number allowed me to record a four-minute outgoing message to explain all about the property and to answer the routine questions right up front. The outgoing message explained financing, the school systems, and everything I could possibly think of about the house. It also prompted the caller to leave a message if they had additional questions. The 800 number captured all the telephone numbers that called, so if I could not understand the message, I had access to the telephone number to return their call. That produced a lot of phone calls, a few appointments, but no buyer. Some critics said that my message was too long as people would not want to listen to a four-minute message. I find that difficult to believe because if you were going to put up money to buy a house, one would think you would want to learn as much as you could. The service also indicated the length of time the caller spent listening to the message. Most callers did not listen to the entire message. Some callers were probably just neighbors curious to see what was the price of rent. Some may have hung up after the floor plan description. If you need four bedrooms and this one only had three, why keep listening?

I also ran ads in the newspaper that said "Lease/Purchase." It named the part of the town the house was in, the sales price, and gave the toll-free number. People could call and listen. Sometimes people are afraid to call and talk to someone because they are afraid they will get pressured into something, but they will call and listen to a message.

I did not try to go into a great deal of detail in the newspaper ads because it cost $100 per weekend for a "basic three-line ad." I thought it was better to have people call and listen to the full message. For instance, if I put in my ad that the house had a full fenced yard, and that was not important to them, I would be spending a lot of money in the paper to tell them it had a fenced yard. Next time I may try a five to six line detailed ad and measure the results. I tried to give basic information and leave the detailed information on the answering machine so they knew exactly what the house had before they made the trip to see it.

My goal was to prequalify people, or let them prequalify themselves on what was in the house and what was available. They could drive by and take a look before we met at the house. I also gave them detailed directions to the house.

Again, I started out with a lease/purchase and ended up going with a rental because of the current economic conditions. If interest rates had not been so low for so long at the end of 2002, a lease/purchase would have been a much easier way to put someone in the house. We tried the lease/purchase for about six weeks. In the last two or three weeks we were also running ads to rent the house. There were times when I had two ads in the paper for the same house—one under Houses to Rent and one under Houses for Sale. They were in two different sections of the newspaper, but for the same house. When we ran the ads for the house to rent, we also included the words "Section 8 okay" so that people who were looking for Section 8 housing knew that we would accept that arrangement. I also made some flyers and distributed them at grocery stores and churches in the area. I changed the sign in the front yard to a FOR RENT sign. I changed the wording to "$1,050 per month, 3 bedrooms, 2½ baths." I took out the 800 number and put in a local telephone number. We had a second phone line in our house so we used that one with an answering machine, and it had a much shorter message. (We thought some people might get turned off by calling an 800 number, thinking they may be dealing with a big corporation, rather than a mom-and-pop-sized company.) If you do not have a second line, use your cell phone. Do not have a cell phone? Get moving into the twenty-first century! Even cartoon characters have cell phones these days.

SHOWING THE HOUSE

When I set up appointments to show the house, I would try to pre-qualify people on the telephone by asking them when they wanted to move, what part of town they were moving from, how many children they had, how many bedrooms they needed, and why they were moving. When I advertised in the newspaper, I would get calls from people from as far away as Ohio. (Remember, I am in Georgia.) I got calls from Tennessee and Ohio from people who were relocating to the area and needed to find housing. They had pulled up the newspaper ads on the Internet. It was interesting that ads in Georgia newspapers are answered from distant states. When I talked to people on the phone, I would tell them about the school system and how the house had been renovated, and we would make an appointment. I made sure to get their telephone number and call them about an hour before the appointment to verify it. I still got stood up 50 percent of the time. You read that right—50 percent of the people who had told me they were coming within an hour of the appointment, never showed up. Welcome to being a landlord! The first couple of times it was a real disappointment. Somehow, learning from others that this is a common problem, that this could happen each time, made it easier to take the next time. So, hopefully you will remember this when you are standing in an empty house all alone.

It was interesting watching the different people who showed up looking for rental housing. I had single moms. I had gay couples. I had young brothers. I had families. I had a divorced dad. One of the most interesting couples who dropped by during an Open House was a handsome couple in a Mercedes looking for a rental house, but they thought my house was too expensive and they were trying to save money. They were driving a Mercedes for which the insurance is astronomical, the maintenance is very high, and so is the high acquisition cost. They had spent a lot of money on something going down in value, which prevented them from buying a house that goes *up* in value. That, to me, was comical, but so prevalent in our society. In his book *Rich Dad, Poor Dad,* Robert Kiyosaki talks about spending your money on things that go up in value. As I am writing this book I am driving an eight-year-old Ford car with 130,000 miles on it because it is paid for and runs every day. The lesson here: Spend your money on things that go *up* in value.

When I set up appointments with prospective renters, I would show up at the house 10 to 15 minutes early, make sure the lights were on around the outside of the house, and remove any trash from the yard. I would go inside the house, turn on the heat, turn on all the lights in the kitchen including the one over the stove, and make sure the water was turned on and running clear. I opened the blinds and drapes to allow as much natural light as possible into the house. I flushed the toilets and scrubbed the watermarks so the bowls looked clean. I also checked to see that no bugs had crawled out from the baseboard after the pest control man had been there. Bugs tend to do that, and die right near the wall. A dead bug is a good bug, but you still do not want to see it.

I got the house in very presentable shape and as prospective renters came in, I would introduce myself, explain the layout, and show the new stove in the kitchen. I would let them explore the bedrooms and bathrooms on their own. Once they had made it back to the master bedroom, I would follow up and point out a few details. I wanted to give them time to themselves so they would not feel constantly pressured. We would walk to the lower level, I would show them where the security system was located and the washer-dryer hookups. This is a pretty standard walk-through for a house. We then would go back to the deck where it was quiet and observe the fenced yard and talk about the money: the rent, deposit, and filling out a credit application. This last conversation took place either on the deck or in the kitchen area.

These are all the different steps I took to finding a tenant. My credit application is a combination between a John Adams credit application and a Heinsite credit application. Heinsite (www. heinsite.com or 770-559-4596) is the name of the company that processes my credit applications, so I get a signature on one of their forms so they can process it. I go into more detail on qualifying the tenant in the next chapter.

I kept several copies of blank credit applications in the rental house. When I met with people I would usually hand them a credit application. Sometimes I would wait to see if they asked for one. Sometimes I put it into their hands and asked them if they would like to sit down and fill it out. I do not know that one way worked better than the other. Just make sure they know that the credit applications are there, and they can fill one out. I also cover that on the telephone before we meet. I ask them to bring a checkbook so they can write a check to Heinsite Services. I emphasize that I do not make a penny on the credit application. Some people think credit applications are money-makers. They believe you make money on credit applications, which you do not. Be sure you get a complete credit application. If they fill one out on the spot, check that the phone number of the current landlord, phone numbers of their job, phone numbers of their references, or their parents or emergency numbers are all listed correctly on the application. You also need a listing of all the people who are going to live in the house. If there will be other adults in the house, you will want to run a criminal check on those individuals for obvious reasons. You deserve to know who is living in your house and what their background is.

WHEN THE RIGHT GUY SHOWED UP—MY FIRST TENANT

I got a call one Saturday morning from a young girl on a cell phone asking questions for her dad—whom I could hear in the background. They were at the house and called the number off the sign. We chatted about two minutes and she said, "Okay," and hung up. I did not even get a chance to ask her name or get her number— *Aaaggghhh*. I thought I let somebody slip through my fingers. I had several people do this before and then never showed up for the appointment so I had become a little skeptical of the whole situation. When I got home from church on Sunday, I found a message from

the same girl to ask to come see the house. We made an appointment to meet at the house (after he got off work) at seven o'clock
Sunday evening. The whole family showed up (my favorite),
walked through the house, talked to me for three minutes asking
general questions and said, "We'll take it—do you have forms or
paperwork to sign?" At this point *shut up and give him the paperwork*. That sounds simple but you would be surprised how many
people keep talking long after the sale is made.

I gave him a credit application; he said he would bring it back
next week with the deposit money. I should have pushed to have
him sit down and fill it out but I had a gut feeling that this guy was
for real. (And he was a good gut feeling!) He had three issues he
wanted to cover.

1. He wanted to buy the house but was starting his own business
   (in the same line as his previous work) and would not be able
   to afford the down payment and qualify to get a mortgage for
   a couple of years. (Great Issue)
2. His credit got messed up when someone stole his checkbook
   last year. (It was a long story and it all made sense—he was
   also a family man and wanted out of an apartment and into a
   house.)
3. He wanted to put in new countertops at *his expense*. I told
   him he should probably wait until he had bought the house to
   spend that kind of money. (Stupid Answer)

We met back at the house the following weekend and he brought
the deposit money, credit application, and a tape measure for the
countertops—turned out his *wife* wanted the new countertops. By
now I had gotten wise to *free* countertops and let him go ahead and
measure to his little heart's content. The countertops that were in
there needed to be replaced anyway so whatever he put in would
be better than what was there. We signed the rent agreement first
and *then* did the inspection. He had no problems with the house in
as-is condition.

How I Landed a Tenant

We went over the list of phone numbers for the utility companies and the move-in date. Since there was a soft rental market at the time, I let him move in two weeks early. This allowed the family two weekends to put in new countertops and move and clean out their old apartment by the end of the month, which was a Thursday. They were thrilled and I got the utilities out of my name two weeks earlier than planned. I treated them the way I wanted to be treated—it is amazing how that works.

His credit was just as he had described it. There were a couple of late payments, but all were confined to one specific time period. His rent had been paid on time for the past three years. You may not find a tenant with perfect credit. I do not require *perfect* credit. I want evidence that they pay their rent first and their credit cards last. I want to know if they have been convicted of a violent crime. One applicant had a DUI eight years ago. That would not restrict me from renting to him. You can deny someone with a criminal background. That will be your judgment call.

In the end I gave away two weeks of rent and got someone else to pay the utilities and install new countertops. I was as much of an answered prayer to him as he was to me.

MOTIVATIONAL QUOTE

Courage is doing what you're afraid to do. There can be no courage unless you're scared.

Eddie Rickenbacher

CHAPTER 12

Qualifying a Tenant

WHY IS IT NECESSARY?

Qualifying a tenant is the first step to getting a *quality* tenant. You do not want someone who is going to constantly battle you over little problems like burned out light bulbs or big problems like dealing drugs out of your house. I was well-advised to never rent a house without thoroughly checking out who is going to live there. You want to do a credit application and a criminal background check, and you want to verify their previous rent paying history. You also want to look for some stability on the job, or at least in the same industry, to ensure that he or she demonstrates both psychological and financial stability. Now, this does not necessarily mean that your potential renters must be rock solid, because if they were, they probably would not be in the rental market! You are looking for somebody who is in a transition or who may never be able to save enough money for a down payment on a house. It is very important to get a criminal background check and credit reports before you allow somebody to live in your house. You are entrusting them with a big investment.

WHAT AM I LOOKING FOR?

I am looking for somebody who has a believable story, is calm, looks me in the eye, and has a clean car. It would be preferably a paid-for car. I want renters who live within their means. I am not looking for perfect credit. They may have collections. These days you will likely see collections from hospitals or doctors' offices, particularly if they have children. They may have had a repossession on a car when they were younger—maybe when they were 26 and now they are 32. Anything in the past seven years will still show up on their report. I am not looking for perfect credit, but I do want to see a pattern that in the past one to two years they have been paying their bills on time, their income has been steady, and they have some consistency on their jobs so they can pay their bills. I also look to see that their bills have not suddenly increased. For example, they may have just bought a new car that has a $400 a month payment and now they cannot afford their $1,100 rent, so they pursue renting your house for $1,000 a month because they think they will save $100 per month and that will solve their money problems. This could be a red flag that they will have trouble making rent on a consistent basis. It is a good sign when they make an appointment around their work schedule. You know they have a job, and it is important to them.

I also want to know how much rent the people are paying now. "Where are you living now? Why are you moving? How much rent are you paying now?" If you own single-family houses, you will find that most of your people are coming from apartments or condominiums. They are coming from someplace where they are crowded or they are living with someone else's family and they want to get a place of their own. They may need a yard and additional storage space. I am looking for a living or financial pattern. I want to know that they have the ability to pay their loans and have consistency in paying their loans or bills on time.

Instant Deal Killers

If somebody told me that they had just filed for bankruptcy, they are being evacuated from their current quarters, they had just lost their job, or had just gotten out of jail (depending on what they did), then any of these things would produce a very difficult credit application to approve. You must have in your mind some things that are going to be instant deal killers for you. I am probably more interested in their criminal background check than I am in the credit report.

THE CREDIT REPORT

I want to make sure that the last year on the credit report is clean, and that prospective tenants are on a path of paying their bills on time. I need to know that their income is steady. In late 2002 and early 2003 we are seeing a large number of corporate layoffs, so I need to know that their income is going to be sufficient. That is one reason people like to rent to people with Section 8 housing because the government pays the rent, or a good portion of it.

Once a prospective renter hands me a completed application, I fax it to Heinsite Services. When you process the application with Heinsite Services, the fee is $35.00, and they do all the work. I ask the prospective tenant to pay the $35.00. A tenant who is truly interested will pay the $35.00 fee. Inevitably you are the one who needs to decide if you want to pay this fee. If every rental house and apartment in the neighborhood has a sign with big bold letters that says *No Application Fee* then you may need to do the same. Since it was my first rental house, I wanted to check everyone who showed interest in the house. It took Heinsite Services about one and a half to two business days to process the application.

Heinsite will then fax or e-mail the person's credit report, their current landlord pay history, and their criminal background check. You could read a complete book on how to read credit reports. It is not an exact science; it is more of an art. Please get a copy of your own credit report as we discuss in Chapter 2. Along with the credit report that you received from the credit bureau you will receive an explanation on how to read credit reports. You will see what they call trade lines. Trade lines are lists of accounts at Sears, J.C. Penney, MasterCard, or Visa. You get the name of the financial institution issuing credit, the current balance, what the limit is, and how many times you may have been 30 days late, 60 days late, or 90 days late. They will then rate each trade line on a scale of one to nine. The scale rates one as the best credit and nine as the worst credit. You can see how many ones they have, and how many twos, threes, and nines and get an overall picture of their credit. Unless you have avoided all consumer help programs for the past five years, you may have heard of credit scores. The credit score is not as important to me as looking at the pattern or time frame of late payments. If somebody has had several 30-day late payments, that is one thing, but if they have had a number of 90-day late payments, that is a whole different story. Here is an overly simplistic example. Let us take John Doe with four 30-day late payments. Okay, he may be slightly irresponsible, and not too concerned with his credit. He may not even understand this is hurting his credit. But in the end he is paying his bills. Now let us look at his brother, who has four 90-day late payments and two charge offs. He just does not like to pay his bills, or often does not have the money.

Any credit card charge off in the past seven years will be on the report. Sam Shopper has a $458 write-off from Tools Are Us (TAU). TAU tried to collect for 18 months with no success, and finally wrote off the $458 debt. This is on his credit report.

Another item you may find is a car repossession. Jane Doe had $4,000 left to pay on her car loan. She was two months behind. She avoided the bank's telephone calls hoping she would find the money in time. Finally, the bank sent the big black tow truck to her house and repossessed her car. Since the bank naturally did not want the car, they sold it as soon as possible at the local auction house. For this example let us say it brought $3,000 at the auction. Technically, Jane is still on the hook for the $1,000 difference between the $3,000 the bank received on the car and the $4,000 she owes. Therefore, the bank will report to the credit bureaus that Jane owes them $1,000 on an automobile loan. To clear this, she will need to pay back the $1,000.

You will have a section in the beginning of the credit report that explains any liens, collections, or judgments. These are descriptions of legal actions taken against the applicant. Sometimes they are as little as $50.00 to the cable company. They may be many thousands of dollars to a hospital. These collections almost paint a picture of the person and their attitude toward paying their bills. Many times you will see on a credit report where, for instance, all their late payments seem to be in mid-1998. "What happened?" you ask. "Well, that was when I got a divorce." Oh yes, that is pretty obvious, or it appears that in May of 1999 they got behind in three different bills. "What happened?" You might get a response that his mother was in the hospital for a month and he was going back and forth to work. "They got tired of me leaving my job so I lost it and my mother died. I did get a job by the end of June and by September I had all my bills caught up." That can be a logical, obvious story, and it was a one-time occurrence.

Any time you have late payments on a credit report you might just say, "What happened?" There may be a very valid explanation. You certainly do not want something like "I just did not get around to paying them." That is not a good explanation! You must remember that this is a business, and you are allowing these people to live in your house. Think of your prospective renters as if you were a corporation and they were a corporation, and you were going to sell them your goods or services on credit. Do you think you will get paid for your goods or services? That is the bottom line. *Are you going to get paid?* Once you sign a lease agreement, or a rental agreement, and you get your deposit, you want to be very emphatic about the rules. This is not a personal relationship. This is business. You tell them that they have to make their payments on time or you will file an eviction notice. "I am not going to wait a week. Your payments are due on the first. At 5:00 P.M. on the first day of the month I am sending out your first notice." Let them know, right up front, the rules of the game. (See Chapter 15 for evictions.)

RENTER PROFILES

Let us talk about different types of renters, the story, the situation, and some different case studies to decide who would be good renters and who would be potentially bad renters. This is not designed to be discriminatory, but simply to allow you to apply some common sense and thought regarding people with different situations who may come walking through your door.

Our favorite renter is a blue-collar worker with no kids who regularly comes home after work (instead of going to the bar). He is tired, sits on the couch, and watches television. That is my favorite renter.

My least favorite renters are groups of twenty-three-year-old guys who have big, loud parties on Friday and Saturday nights and tear up the house. Somewhere in between you will find all the other stories.

Let us start out with couples with kids: Mom and Dad and a couple of kids. A very typical scenario is they will make good renters because they have two sources of income. The down side is they may be trying to get ahead in life, and with two sources of income they will be saving for a down payment to buy a house. We may talk to them about purchasing the rental house on a Lease/Purchase, or understand that they may well not be there five years from now. With two sources of income, depending on what job skills they have, they may be saving money for a down payment to get into a house of their own. The down side with two kids is that they tend to be hard on a house. Crayon marks on walls, hot wheel cars running across the kitchen floor and marking up the trim, lots of spilled stuff on the carpet—stuff kids do. It is the stuff I did when I was a kid, and so did you. You just need to be aware of the wear and tear that kids will put on a house. The same thing applies to pets. They are hard on a house. So I would most like to have a blue-collar worker with a wife and no kids or pets. (Yeah, and I would like to win the lottery, too!)

Let us talk about single moms. I see a lot of them with kids. Some are on Section 8 housing vouchers, some are self-sufficient, and some are getting a divorce and need to move out of their current apartment or house. If Mom has child support and depends on it to make the rent and utility payments, you are entitled to get 12 months cancelled checks and read the divorce decree to see if and how long payments will continue. I like to have Moms come and look at the house with the kids. Sometimes people come into the house and leave their kids in the car. Other times the kids come into the house and run through the house like wild things. I do not get too excited about that. However, I do like to have the kids come in with Mom so I can see how they behave. Many times the kids will tell you a lot about the parents. I have been talking to other landlords, and they always encourage me to talk to the kids. Kids will tell you things like, "My daddy punched a hole in the wall in our last house. Our landlord told us we have to move so that is why we are here today." Be nice to the kids and engage them in conversation. They may have a world of insight that the parents do not volunteer.

Divorced dads. Newly separated dads that do not have a final divorce decree make me a little nervous because they do not know how much alimony they are going to have to pay (assuming they do not have custody of the children). I have two buddies who did get custody of their children so it's not like it used to be. They are just moving out and getting separated. Usually, you have a large unknown payment that is going to enter into their lives called "child support and alimony." Just be very cautious and run the financial numbers to make sure Dad can afford both your house and the alimony payments at the same time.

John Adams has a great audiocassette tape called *Top Ten Mistakes that Landlords Make.* You can log on his web site at www.money99.com and order that tape. He goes through some of the different scenarios as well. He has some additional thoughts on other people whom he tries to avoid renting to. You cannot discriminate on race, color, religion, national origin, age, gender, marital status, or receipt of income from public assistance programs. Bad credit and criminal behavior is not discrimination. You can certainly deny someone from living in your house for having bad credit, or if their income is not stable enough. One suggestion is that when someone comes to the house, excuse yourself to get something out of your car. Try to go outside and look into the car of the person who is there. Many times, if their car is clean they will keep the house clean. If their car is messy and full of stuff their house is probably messy, too. It is also a good idea to write down the license plate numbers so if you have any problems, you have the license plate number of the people who came to see you.

VERIFY THE FUNDS

Once you get the deposit check and first month's rent you can call the bank and "verify funds." The bank will ask you for the checking account number and the amount and then tell you whether they have the funds to pay that check *today.* It does not mean they will have the funds three days from now when the check gets there. You can also go to the bank and ask to have the check converted to a cashier's check (certified funds). The bank may charge you $5.00 to $20.00 to do this but you will know your check is good before you let tenants move in. My rent agreement specifies that if a check is returned for insufficient funds, it will cost the tenant $50.00. See Chapter 12 for more on rent agreements.

INSPECTION

Before a tenant moves in you need to do a move-in inspection. You need to go through each room and specify if there are any holes in the walls, any nicks in the drywall, a mark on the ceiling, or if the light fixture is chipped or cracked so that when people move out you can make accurate records and charge their security deposit accordingly. This is for their protection as well as your own.

CHAPTER 13

Protecting Your Investment with the Right Lease Agreements

You have bought your first rental house and are ready to make money from your new investment! You have interviewed several prospective tenants and it seems you have found the right one. Now what? How do you go about getting a bona fide commitment from a tenant while protecting your own interests? The key is to use a strong lease agreement.

WHAT MAKES A GOOD LEASE AGREEMENT?

In its most simplistic terms a good lease agreement lays out all the ground rules of how the relationship of landlord and tenant is to be guided. I like the thought that the thicker, the better. The more you have in your lease, the easier it will be to enforce those rules down the road. It is very difficult, if not impossible, to enforce a verbal lease, particularly after 12 months. There is a web site that lists all the different restrictions for each of the 50 states. The web site is www.nolo.com/lawcenter/statute/state.cfm. That will take you to a list of all the state laws. Another web site is www.findlaw.com/public.html. Those two web sites will help you find answers to specific questions before you start locating an attorney. I used a rental agreement that I had purchased as part of a $100 kit called The Landlord Survival Guide (kit contains book, audiocassette tape, and floppy disk full of forms) from John Adams at www.money99.com that he calls his "killer lease" because it is very detailed and covers 35 different topics. Since it is a copyrighted document I cannot publish it here, but I can highlight and summarize some of the most important points.

The Front Page

On the front page, make sure you include the following:

- The name of the manager or management company.
- The address of the property.
- Who the resident(s) is/are.
- What appliances are supplied with the house. (In my case the appliances included water heater, furnace, air-conditioner, dishwasher, and gas stove.)
- The initial term with the beginning date, the termination date, and the monthly rate.
- Any discount for paying on the first day of the month and how they may qualify for that discount.
- The security deposit, a nonrefundable pet deposit, and specifications of what pets are allowed, if any.

The Rent

Use an agreement that is very specific in how it describes the rent, any discounts that may be available, and any late fees. Each one of these in the John Adams lease is spelled out separately. Anything about the money needs to be very detailed with no questions left unanswered about how this is to be run. This includes a statement that the resident shall pay a $50.00 return check fee if their check is returned for insufficient funds. You need this spelled out in the lease up front. Otherwise, you risk potentially costly misunderstandings. Understand that when you go to court, the judge can enforce only what the tenant has agreed to. You want the utilities specified as to which name (yours or the renter's) utilities would be listed in. When I moved my tenants into my house, I had a checklist for them of the utility companies names, the date on which I would have them turned off in my name, and the date that tenants could have them turned on in their name. This way, both parties are clear.

Property Use and Maintenance

You want to have a paragraph on how the property is to be used—namely, as a family dwelling. You do not want to have people selling drugs out of your house, turning your rental property into a bed-and-breakfast house, or subleasing the house to tenants of their own. Also spell out who is responsible for maintenance, repairs, and alterations. Be very specific as to what alterations your tenants can and cannot perform to your property.

Property Inspections

You want to have access to the property for inspections. When I told my tenant that I would inspect the property every 60 days, or as needed, I explained that I would merely be inspecting the property for maintenance issues such as leaky water under the sink or around tubs or windows, or if I had a leaky roof. I stressed that I would be looking for maintenance issues and did not care if the sink was full of dirty dishes or the kids' clothes were piled up in their rooms. That does not bother me at all. I want access to the house because I want to look for the $ 0.50 maintenance items before they become $500 renovation items, and I also want to determine that the tenants do not have 50 people living in the house or two big German shepherd dogs living in the house and tearing up the carpet. I explained to the tenant up front what I would be looking for when I did my inspections, and what I would not be looking for so the tenant understood fully. He thought the inspections were a good idea.

Liability Issues

You want to specify your indemnification that the management should not be liable for any damage or injury to the resident so that when people slip and fall on the proverbial banana peel on the front steps, they cannot sue you for it. In our lawsuit-happy society you need to be very specific in what you are responsible for and what you are not.

Right to Increase Rent

An escalation clause says that the management has the right to increase the rent during the term of the lease with a 30-, 60-, or 90-day written notice to the resident. This allows you to increase the rent to the tenant one year from that date.

Eviction Process

You need to specify the eviction proceedings. If the rent has not been received by the fifth day of the month, you have the right to assert all contractual remedies to enforce the lease. You specify in your lease on what day you will begin eviction proceedings because when you go before the judge and say the tenant has not paid you, he will want to see the contract that the tenant signed.

Early Termination

Mention in your contract "Early Termination," which states how a tenant can get out of their lease early, what they are responsible for, and what they are not responsible for.

Insurance Coverage

You need to inform them that they should have renters insurance, possibly giving them phone numbers of some agents who sell it. I urge you to have your tenants get renters insurance to protect their belongings. If you have a broken water pipe in your house, management or the owners will be responsible for fixing the water pipe. They would not, however, be responsible for replacing the damaged stereo that belonged to the tenant. That would be covered under their renters insurance. Specify who is responsible for telephones and smoke detectors. You need to state that the tenant is prohibited from changing or adding additional locks on the doors without consent of the management/owner. You need to know that your key always fits the door. Also, you need to know who is responsible for any pest control. These are some of the issues that will make a good lease arrangement.

Move-In Inspection

You want to have a "move-in" inspection list that mentions any marks on the linoleum or drywall or if there is a droopy spot on the ceiling because it leaked five years ago. You may have fixed the roof, but did not bother to fix the ceiling. Small details all around the property would be on the move-in inspection list that would allow you to compare the property at the time the tenants move out. You want the current tenant to pay for those items that are above normal wear and tear when they move out that were not on the move-in list. If they punched a hole in the wall, they need to pay for that. If you start to notice that the ceiling has a soft spot or sags in a particular place, that will alert you to a possible leak in the roof that has developed in the past 6 or 12 months that was not there at the beginning. This list can alert you to other maintenance issues that you should be aware of. A move-in section list is very important because it protects you and your security deposit as well as the tenants' when they move out.

WHERE DO YOU FIND LEASE AGREEMENTS?

There are several places where you can get lease templates. I got mine from www.money99.com. If you order the Carlton Sheets course, it comes with a lease. A real estate investors association in your area may also have sample leases.

Web Resources

An Internet site www.nolo.com has several books on creating a solid residential lease. There are two books by Attorney Janet Portman, Marcia Stewart and Attorney Ralph Warner called *Lease Writer* for $59.95 and *Every Landlord's Legal Guide* for $38.00 that cover the rental legalities every landlord needs to know including tenant selections, security deposits, writing leases and rental agreements, repairs, maintenance, and much more.

You can also go to www.hud.com. There are a number of places that will give you sample lease agreements. Other resources for obtaining a lease are at www.thelpa.com (Landlord Protection Agency) and http://landlordtenanthelp.com. It is very important that you have a good lease agreement because you have to be prepared to follow through with the consequences if your tenant breaks the lease. That is why the thicker, the better for the lease. The more detailed it is, the better protected you are as the landlord when the tenants attempt to break the lease. It must be very specific as to what they can and cannot do, and it makes your relationship better and easier. Spending time up front creating a good lease agreement is well worth the time and effort and saves frustration down the road.

Landlord–Tenant Codes

To help you research your state laws, here is a listing of landlord–tenant codes for the 50 states. Because landlord–tenant laws vary significantly depending on where you live, it is important to check your state and local laws for specifics. Here are some of the key statutes pertaining to landlord–tenant laws in each state. To find these statutes, visit Nolo.com's Legal Research Center at http://www.nolo.com/lawcenter/statute/state.cfm.

Alabama	Ala. Code §§ 35-9-1 to 100
Alaska	Alaska Stat. §§ 34.03.010 to .380
Arizona	Ariz. Rev. Stat. Ann. §§ 12-1171 to 1183; §§ 33-1301 to 1381
Arkansas	Ark. Code Ann. §§ 18-16-101 to 306
California	Cal. [Civ.] Code §§ 1925-1954, 1961-1962.7, 1995.010-1997.270
Colorado	Colo. Rev. Stat. §§ 38-12-101 to 104, 301 to 302
Connecticut	Conn. Gen. Stat. Ann. §§ 47a-1 to 51
Delaware	Del. Code Ann. tit. 25, §§ 5101-7013
District of Columbia	D.C. Code Ann. §§ 42-3201 to 4097, 3501.01 to 3509.03
Florida	Fla. Stat. Ann. §§ 83.40-.66
Georgia	Ga. Code Ann. §§ 44-7-1 to 81
Hawaii	Haw. Rev. Stat. §§ 521-1 to 78
Idaho	Idaho Code §§ 6-301 to 324 and §§ 55-201 to 313

Illinois	Ill. Comp. Stat. ch. 765 para. 705/0.01-740/5
Indiana	Ind. Code Ann. §§ 32-7-1-1 to 37-7-9-10
Iowa	Iowa Code Ann. §§ 562A.1-.36
Kansas	Kan. Stat. Ann. §§ 58-2501 to 2573
Kentucky	Ky. Rev. Stat. Ann. §§ 383.010-.715
Louisiana	La. Rev. Stat. Ann. §§ 9:3201-:3259; La. Civ. Code Ann. art. 2669-2742
Maine	Me. Rev. Stat. Ann. tit. 14, §§ 6001-6046
Maryland	Md. Real Prop. Code Ann. §§ 8-101 to 604
Massachusetts	Mass. Gen. Laws Ann. ch. 186 §§ 1-21
Michigan	Mich. Comp. Laws Ann. § 554.601-.640
Minnesota	Minn. Ann. Stat. §§ 504B.001 to 504B.471
Mississippi	Miss. Code Ann. §§ 89-8-1 to 27
Missouri	Mo. Ann. Stat. §§ 441.005 to .880 and §§ 535.150-.300
Montana	Mont. Code Ann. §§ 70-24-101 to 25-206
Nebraska	Neb. Rev. Stat. §§ 76-1401 to 1449
Nevada	Nev. Rev. Stat. Ann. §§ 118A.010-.520
New Hampshire	N.H. Rev. Stat. Ann. §§ 540:1 to 540:29; 540-A:1-540-A:8
New Jersey	N.J. Stat. Ann. §§ 46:8-1 to 49
New Mexico	N.M. Stat. Ann. §§ 47-8-1 to 51
New York	N.Y. Real Property Law ("RPL") §§ 220-238; Real Property Actions and Proceedings Law ("RPAPL")§§ 701-853; Multiple Dwelling Law ("MDL") all; Multiple Residence Law ("MRL") all; General Obligation Law ("GOL") §§ 7-103-108

North Carolina	N.C. Gen. Stat. §§ 42-1 to 42-14.2; 42-25-6 to 42-76
North Dakota	N.D. Cent. Code §§ 47-16-01 to 41
Ohio	Ohio Rev. Code Ann. §§ 5321.01-.19
Oklahoma	Okla. Stat. Ann. tit. 41, §§ 1-136
Oregon	Or. Rev. Stat. §§ 90.100-.450
Pennsylvania	Pa. Stat. Ann. tit. 68, §§ 250.101-.510-B
Rhode Island	R.I. Gen. Laws §§ 34-18-1 to 57
South Carolina	S.C. Code Ann. §§ 27-40-10 to 910
South Dakota	S.D. Codified Laws Ann. §§ 43-32-1 to 29
Tennessee	Tenn. Code Ann. §§ 66-28-101 to 520
Texas	Tex. Prop. Code Ann. §§ 91.001-92.354
Utah	Utah Code Ann. §§ 57-17-1 to 5, 22-1 to 6
Vermont	Vt. Stat. Ann. tit. 9, §§ 4451-4468
Virginia	Va. Code Ann. §§ 55-218.1 to 248.40
Washington	Wash. Rev. Code Ann. §§ 59.04.010-.900, .18.010-.911
West Virginia	W. Va. Code §§ 37-6-1 to 30
Wisconsin	Wis. Stat. Ann. §§ 704.01-.45
Wyoming	Wyo. Stat. §§ 1-21-1201 to 1211; 34-2-128 to 129

CHAPTER 14

What to Expect When Becoming a Landlord

What keeps people from fulfilling their dream of owning rental property? It is usually fear, that is, fear of the unknown. But what if you had a clear idea of what to expect, *before* you took the plunge? Wouldn't that make the process much less daunting for you? That is what this chapter is designed to do—to give you a heads up to help you anticipate and prepare to succeed in the days ahead. Here are 10 things to expect as you embark on buying your first rental house.

Expect to be nervous. Face it. You are going to have massive butterflies in your stomach. Your hands will shake when you sign the sales contract. You will walk out of the closing attorney's office and feel a pit in your stomach. You are taking a risk, and with that risk comes fear of loss. Treat the anxiety you feel as something that is part of playing the game, and do not allow it to impede your success. Think about all the stages of life that have brought you to this point in your life. For example, I was nervous the first time I drove a car. I was nervous the first time I signed the papers to buy a car. I was nervous when I closed on a primary residence for the first time (the home I lived in, not the house I rented). I remember waking up in that home the first morning and thinking "I cannot afford this home." I was petrified when we brought our first daughter home from the hospital.

Now, buying and driving a car is routine, something I take for granted. We have since been to the closing table for refinances and additional home purchases and I do not lose a bit of sleep. And that second daughter, well she was a walk in the park—I highly recommend having the second child first—you are much calmer!!

I can already feel that the next house will be so much easier—significantly less emotional. Since my plan is to buy 2 houses each year for the next 10 years, I expect the closing attorney's office to become routine, also.

Expect to make mistakes. And do not fear making them! You are new at this rental house thing. So why expect to be a seasoned real estate mogul at the outset? You know, our educational system causes us to associate great pain with making mistakes. And this is a shame. The truth is the only people who do not make mistakes are the people who do not accomplish anything. Listen! Mistakes can be good and quite frankly, no matter how bright you are, you are going to make them. So get over it! You will make mistakes in writing contracts. You will make mistakes in making offers. You will make mistakes when you talk to sellers. Just make sure you *learn* from your errors and not repeat them! The number one mistake you want to avoid is paying too much for a house.

Think about all the mistakes you made while learning to walk or ride a bicycle. I still have scars on my left knee!! You know those daughters I spoke of previously? My wife and I will make countless mistakes during child rearing in the years to come. Compared to raising our daughters, the rental properties are not nearly the risk! In other words, there are other things to be more nervous about. Put it in perspective—what is the worst thing that can happen? You could lose some money. Losing money is not fun, but sometimes it may be necessary to learn the lessons of life. Think how much money people spend on a college education—and that does not guarantee financial stability.

Do not freak out on me here! The plan here is to *make* money. Be careful; do not let the possibility of losing money overshadow the probability of making money.

Expect to spend a lot of time reviewing a lot of properties. This is one way to help you minimize mistakes! I encourage you to study at least 20 houses before you make your first offer. You will know the area and the average condition of the house you are going into versus what is on the market. In the books and stories I read in preparing for this project, a common mistake people make is that they buy the second house they look at. They do not do enough research on the area and they overpay for their property. Chapter 14 details a time line of my first deal—it does not include all the research on previous deals. This deal has been a long time coming.

Expect expenses to be more than you think. While optimism is a must-have trait for real estate entrepreneurs, it does not serve you well when projecting financial requirements. The best-case scenario rarely happens on your first deal. Surprise expenses, late payments from tenants, and lower-than-anticipated rent proceeds can all kill your dreams if you do not account for surprises in your projections.

You also need to expect that computing your personal income taxes and tax analysis are going to be somewhat complicated on a rental house, because not only do you have the purchase price of the house, and the capital gains and appreciation on the house, but you also have income and expenses, so it affects your income statement and balance sheet differently. In other words, your income statement shows your income minus expenses. Expenses are such items as advertising or insurance. They are not new furniture or a new roof. That has to do with a capital expenditure or a gain or loss on the cost basis of the house. If you bought the house for $100,000 and spent $3,000 on a new roof, the cost of that house is now $103,000. If you sell it later for $110,000 you had a gain of $7,000. Therefore, some of your expenses are going to be attributed to capital gains costs on the cost basis of the house, and some of your expenses will be on your annual income statement on your taxes.

To keep yourself—and your numbers—in check, find someone with whom you can be accountable, perhaps a CPA, mentor, or business partner. When you balance your optimism with sober thinking, you ensure you will have the means to keep yourself in business for the long haul.

Expect to negotiate.   First, let me say "I hate haggling over prices," so do not haggle. Negotiate. Haggling is arguing over 50-cent oranges in Jamaica. Negotiating is making a win-win situation for two people with different sets of problems. One wants to sell and one wants to buy. Both of you want the best deal and want to close quickly. If you do not learn to love negotiating, you will inevitably pay too much and put yourself in a money-losing position. With that said, do not be afraid to place low-ball offers. Those are the only offers that you want accepted! Just because it is a low-ball offer does not mean it is not a win-win deal. Their win may be a quick closing and your win is value. You will probably make 20 or 30 offers before you get one accepted. If you find that a house you low-balled six months ago is still on the market, make the same offer again. When people first put their house on the market, they may think it is worth, say, $150,000, but after it sits for six to nine months, they may be very willing to take $125,000 or even $110,000. This is especially true if they have been making mortgage payments during that period of time. Just because somebody says no today, does not mean they will say no forever!

Expect to deal with all types of people—the good, the bad, and the ugly.
You need to have people skills in negotiating deals, working with

contractors, showing prospective tenants your house, talking about money, and collecting rents. You do not need the verbal skills of a talk show host but be pleasant, sincere, and to the point with people. Be prepared to work with people of different cultures, religions, races, and backgrounds. We are all in this for *green* money. I do not care if they have dyed their hair blue (which I saw), as long as they pay their rent on time and take care of our house. I had to continually remind myself not to judge a book by its cover. Someone may look like the perfect tenant and in reality be just a smooth talker. That friend who promises to be a good contractor may not ever show up. I wish there were a test you could give people to determine how you will get along. Sorry—no test.

Remember my carpet cleaner story? When the first contractor turned out to be a jerk, I called another guy who worked out to be fabulous. It was as if he and I were supposed to work together. That is one name that is written in ink in my contact book. There are about 300,000,000 people in the United States—you just need to find 100 people (agents, bankers, tenants, contractors) to do business. You can expect to go through some situations that would be perfect for *Candid Camera*. Laugh it off and keep going. The carpet cleaner turned out to be a great story at dinner parties.

Expect to spend ample time and money on repairs.   Depending on the condition of your rental house, you will need to spend several weeks getting it ready for show time. If you are going to spend six or seven Saturdays, you need to plan that with your family and your social calendar. I recommend having a family meeting to discuss the time line and strategy. In our case I first got the complete support of my wife. After all, she would be in charge of the girls while I worked on the house. My wife and I explained to the girls why we were buying this house. Initially they thought we were moving into this house and they did not like the idea (we had moved a year ago). You can understand what six- and eight-year-olds were thinking. Why buy a house you were not going to move into? This was a great educational opportunity for everyone in the family. We explained rent, appreciation, mortgages, foreclosure, and the value of a home. I do not know how much they understood, but it will be a continuing education they will not get in school. Take full advantage of it.

There is a funny quote about traveling—Lay out all your clothes and all your money, then take half the clothes and twice the money. I have a friend who is an architect who always has a contingency factor in his budgets to cover the items he never remembers.

As you read in Chapter 9, you should expect to have expenses and repairs you cannot initially prepare for. Some problems are not visible until you get halfway into the renovation.

Expect to make money (but not necessarily quickly). Is it possible to get rich quick in real estate? Define *quick*! This is more of a 10-year plan not a 10-month plan. Do not let quick money be your sole expectation. Otherwise you risk getting discouraged and making rash decisions that could cost you a lot of money. Instead, look at your real estate venture as a long-term business, something you want to build and cultivate over time to make you very wealthy. Then, if you happen to strike it big early, that is gravy! Either way, position yourself for long-term success.

Expect the value of your rental houses to fluctuate over time— economies go in cycles. We all know the stock market fluctuates— but people *have* to have a place to live. That is why I am determined to stay in the smaller houses. People prefer the privacy and family atmosphere of houses to apartments.

Expect emotional ups and downs. I got all pumped up because one day I lined up three families to see the house. Then, no one showed up (actually happened). I mean no one. Another time I thought I had found the ideal renter. She loved the condition of the house, it was clean, and her children would not have to change schools. She filled out an application, paid her fee, and talked about when she could move in. However, the next day she called and said the closets were too small; she was no longer interested (actually happened). I looked at cancelled appointments as part of my time investment—it is part of the job. I did not take it personally and neither should you.

Or you are almost finished getting your house ready to rent when a couple pipes burst in the crawl space, and you have just incurred another major repair expense! How do you cope? Get used to it, and do not take it personally. You will experience ups and downs. That is simply a part of succeeding in any business. Just take it in stride and know that even the most savvy real estate investors experience this. What separates the successful investors from the wannabes is that they have learned to expect the ups and downs and do not allow themselves to get too high or too low, but stay focused on the tasks at hand.

Expect you will need help. As we talk about in Chapter 3, you really need to build a winning team of professionals and mentors to help you succeed for the long haul. These folks can help you navigate around and overcome challenges that could cost you money if you are new at this. By tapping the expertise of successful people in the real estate business, you will save yourself a lot time, money, and heartache in building your own real estate venture!

Continue to attend educational seminars on landlording, property selection, and tax accounting (such as a software program called QuickBooks). One accountant I interviewed for my personal business warned me that some people spend as much as $5,000 in seminars and never buy a house, while others just fly by the seat of their pants. I was more in the middle—well, maybe the cheap side of the middle!

MOTIVATIONAL QUOTE

No man ever achieved worthwhile success who did not, at one time or other, find himself with at least one foot hanging well over the brink of failure.

Napolean Hill

CHAPTER 15

Timeline

I did not know at the time I was buying my first rental house that I would be writing a book, so some of these dates are approximations.

6–1–02   Nan and I spent many hours on the Internet looking at houses. We seldom used www.realtor.com because we have a couple of local sites that we preferred. To find local sites, look at real estate signs in the neighborhoods where you are interested in buying a house. You may also go to a search engine like www.ask.com or www.google.com and search for the real estate company name. For example, you know a large realtor in your area is Investorreal (fictitious name). Go to the search engine and type in the question box Investorreal. If you get too many hits (matches) you can narrow the search. A hit will occur any time those words you typed appear in the web site, even if they are not typed together. For example, you would narrow your search by adding your state or city. The next search would be Investorreal, Florida. This will pull a hit for every site with Investorreal and Florida. There will be a huge volume because it will pull all Investorreal *and* Florida. However, web sites with both words will come up as priority hits. If you do not have access to the Internet at your residence, check your local public library. Usually, this is a free service. There are also businesses that have access to the Internet. Kinko's is a 24-hour copy center that also has Internet access. You can locate your nearest store at www.kinkos.com.

6–1–02   We looked at price, location, and schools. We became familiar with neighborhoods. We knew the area fairly well because we had lived in that county for 12 years. We logged many miles on the car just getting a feel for our target areas.

6–10–02   Applied for and received a preapproval letter to buy an investment house. Also acquired equity line of credit on current home. See Chapter 8 for more details on financing.

6–10–02   Tried to buy a Fannie Mae foreclosure about 25 minutes north of my house. The house was in overall great shape. I did see two things that needed immediate attention:

1. It needed to have the above ground swimming pool removed. This is not a deal breaker, however. Since you never want a pool at a single family rental house, it would require additional labor. There is a market for used above ground pools. Think about what is needed before jumping in with a pool. You

will need to advertise either in the local paper or with flyers. Why do I want the pool out so badly? *Liability*. You, as owner of the property, will take on the liability of a pool that you have no control over on a daily basis.

2. The dishwasher leaked all over the kitchen floor when I inspected it (remember to flush the toilets and run the dishwasher!). Deal breaker? No, but it was a factor to consider. What could be involved? The worst case scenario is potential floor damage and you may have to replace the dishwasher. Therefore, factor that cost into your offer.

Fannie Mae would not budge on the price, and I passed. I looked at several other houses on paper this week. One agent I was working with wanted to make a bunch of low-ball offers without looking at the properties and have the offer include a three-day inspection clause to get out of the contract if I wanted to. This sounded very good on paper—but it did not seem to work in the real world. Nobody took the offers seriously. I later saw this same agent showing somebody the house that I bought *after* I had a signed contract. He was too late to the show.

6–14–02   Tommy Blackwell (real estate agent) called me to come that day to see a house that was *just* listed by an agent in his office. He told me this was the real deal—I should be prepared to make an offer if I really wanted in the game. The location was good for us. It was about 30–40 minutes from our home. This was important since I would do much of the work myself, and would be showing the house to prospective renters.

6–17–02   I took my wife and children to see the house. We made an offer for $98,000. Signed the papers on the tailgate of Tommy's pickup truck. I was shaking like a leaf—at least on the inside. I never thought we would get the house so it was more of a game at this point. The list price was $116,000. We knew we should offer less than list. But how much? Tommy had the listings of current properties and recent sales. We started with a conservative guesstimate from his information, added in the rehab costs, and worked the numbers backwards. We offered $98,000.

6–20–02　We received a call that our offer had not even been reviewed. We were told we might get a response after the month's end. In the mortgage business the last week of the month has a flurry of activity as people want to close and move. We were expecting to hear something in July—maybe even after the Fourth, which was a Thursday in 2002. We didn't expect to hear anything until Monday, July 8.

6–25–02　We got a call that the bank was countering our offer with $101,000. After a little discussion my wife looked at me and said, "Do you want it or not—there is no real difference between 98 and 101." She had this look in her eye I will never forget—it was time to either fish or cut bait (Southern for "time to make a decision"). I had found "the first deal" and I was *scared*. If I passed on this deal I could tell she did not want to get dragged around town for lesser deals. She knew this was right—I knew I was in over my head. We accepted $101,000. I knew I had lit a fuse I could not blow out. I was in the game. We faxed sales contracts with lots of handwritten corrections back and forth. I was calm on the outside and scared on the inside.

6–27–02　We signed the final "pretty" sales contract for $101,000. I also gathered all my documentation and applied for our loan.

Timeline

7–05–02   Appraisal completed. That's right. Friday, July 5 the appraiser was working! I was thrilled to know it appraised for $122,000—which is what we expected, but it is still comforting to see it in black and white from the appraiser.

7–17–02   Wood infestation report—(termite report) it did not have any—that is *good*! It had plenty of other bugs but no termites.

7–22–02   Original closing date—later delayed due to a technicality with the seller providing clear title. This delay is not unusual in foreclosed real estate.

7–29–02   Went to the closing attorney and signed my life away—at least it felt that way! We bought the house from foreclosure. It appraised for $122,000, and we paid $101,000. The loan amount was $97,600 and since I put $1,000 deposit in with the sales contract, and had about $1,000 to pay in county taxes and other minor closing costs, I had $3,400 due at closing. I was actually pretty calm at this point. Looking back at the HUD-1 (closing statement) I saw that the seller paid $8,800 at closing—almost $6,000 of that was sales commission.

8–3–02   Started seven weeks of renovations—mostly Saturdays. My muscles and knees were sore most Sundays! I tried to get materials Thursdays and Fridays so I could work on Saturday. I tried to avoid the big home improvement stores on the weekends when the lines are so long and it is difficult to get any questions answered.

9–1–02   First loan payment due—paid it with my equity line of credit.

9–10–02   Finished renovations and had the carpets steam cleaned. I walked through the house three times and just looked at it. I could not wipe the smile off my face. I couldn't believe how much better it looked. It was fun to review the before and after pictures.

9–14–02 Ran the first ad in the paper—for lease/purchase. I got several calls and showed the house several times but nobody signed the papers.

9–25–02 Refinanced the house—pulled $21,176 cash out. Paid myself back the down payment, the repair costs, and banked the rest. Because I pulled the cash out, this increased my loan amount and made my monthly positive cash flow smaller to the point of breakeven, but I already had the cash in hand—tax-free. I could have elected to have a smaller loan amount—and a bigger monthly cash flow. I may do some of those in the future.

10–1–02 No mortgage payment due because we had refinanced at the end of September.

11–1–02 First mortgage payment on permanent 30-year loan due.

11–2–02 Started advertising the house For Rent. I received a number of calls and showed the house several times but nobody signed the papers.

11–9–02 I attended an all day seminar on Landlording through the Georgia Real Estate Investor's Association. This was very educational and well worth the money (about $100).

1–11–03 Got a call from current tenant to see the house.

1–12–03 Showed the house and he said, "I'll take it—where do I sign the papers?"

1–16–03 Called prospective tenant to make sure he was still coming back on Sunday to sign the lease and give me the deposit.

Timeline

1–18–03 Got a call from the tenant asking if he could meet me Saturday night at 8:00 P.M. instead of Sunday night to give me the money. I thought I could work that into my schedule. My wife did not mind my going out on a Saturday night by myself as long as I came home with $1,000!! I remember sleeping pretty well that night.

2–15–03 Tenant paid rent and moved in.

3–1–03 Started looking for the next house.

3–15–03 Attended a Saturday morning seminar to learn more skills in locating houses. Always learning. Log on to www.firstrentalhouse.com to sign up for my free newsletter. You can see a list of book stores where I will be giving a seminar and signing books.

CHAPTER 16

Getting Paid on Time

If you are going to succeed in making money in rental properties, you need to ensure that you get paid—on time! Otherwise, you risk cash flow problems that can damage your credit and impair your ability to acquire more rental properties.

I have heard of landlords who inconsistently or poorly deal with late and nonpayment of rents. Why people allow someone to live in their house for four months without paying rent is beyond me. It does happen. The laws are different from state to state so be sure to check with your local real estate investors club or an attorney for your state's specific laws. The key to minimizing your exposure is to have a good lease and back it up with properly drafted letters and legal action. Do not be a landlord if you are not prepared to *demand* your rent money. A tenant that does not pay his or her rent is stealing from you!

The overall process of eviction goes pretty quickly if done

properly. The price of speed is accuracy. If the landlord skips steps along the way, then he has to go back to the beginning and start over. Let me repeat—*The price of speed is accuracy.*

Think of all the apartment complexes you pass on the way to work every day or in your daily travels, and think that each one of those may have 400–1,000 or more apartments in them. Now think about how few times you have seen a tenant's belongings carried out to the street. Eviction does not actually happen as often as we all dread it might. It should happen rarely if we select and qualify our tenants properly. That being said we will always have people who either get divorced, lose their jobs, overspend, and undersave. In our society of buy today and pay tomorrow we always have people who do not save money for a rainy day. So for those people, here is how eviction works.

HOW EVICTION WORKS

Please note that this works in my state with a rental agreement that is designed and worked to follow this example.

First Day of the Month

Rent is due by 5:00 P.M. If rent is not paid I will go to the post office box with a fill-in–the-blank late letter and send a late payment letter. You may even have an imaginary secretary or accounting manager, who sends the letter to take the heat off you. The discount rent is not allowed after this date. The rent is not technically due until the fifth but to get the discount rent it must be paid by the first. Be prepared to send a late notice on this day. Call the tenant to tell them the late notice was mailed. By using a post office box you avoid using your home address; therefore the tenant does not know where you live. This is a business. How often do you have a business meeting in your home? For most of us, the answer is never; treat your business with the respect it deserves. The post office will accept mail in their boxes Monday through Friday 8:30 A.M. to 5:00 P.M. and until noon on Saturday. The tenants may take their rent payment there—do not let them take it to your home—otherwise they may be there for an hour telling you why they are late.

If you do not send late notices consistently, then you have in effect granted your tenant a waiver. A waiver says they do not have to abide by the lease since the landlord did not enforce it. You must be consistent and keep copies of all notices sent.

Fifth Day of the Month

If you have not received the rent by the fifth, something is probably wrong. Call the tenant. Send a demand notice. Georgia law requires landlords to formally make demand for the property before they file for eviction. The rent has to be late before you can send a demand letter. Sending this on the first day of the month is a *no-no*.

Sixth Day of the Month

Tack and mail. This is the same system that the sheriff's department uses—mail one copy to the tenant and thumbtack one copy to the front door. You have made an honest effort to contact the tenants about their late payment. If they try to make you feel bad for demanding rent—turn it around on them. "If you do not pay the rent, the owner cannot pay the mortgage, the house will go into foreclosure, and you will be forced out by the bank."

Ninth Day of the Month

File for a dispossessory warrant for nonpayment of rent with the Magistrate Court. For about $50.00 you will have the sheriff (usually a big man carrying a loaded gun) deliver a note to your tenant. The folks at the magistrate clerk's office can help you fill out this relatively simple form. It states:

- Name of the landlord.
- Name of the tenant (s).
- Grounds for eviction.
- That the landlord demanded possession and has been refused.
- The amount of the rent or other money owed.

If you made it through a loan closing, you can make it through this! You can dismiss the dispossessory warrant at any time, but you have to file it if you want to eventually evict your tenant. You cannot get to second base without stepping on first base. The sheriff will use the same tack and mail procedure you used on the fifth and sixth of the month. This process is called "getting service" and gives your tenant seven days to answer in writing to the court. If the tenant cannot write, he/she can tell his answer to the clerk, and he will write it down for them. Do you think your tenant will be taking you seriously at this point? All you have done is sent some letters, filled out a form, and had the *sheriff* deliver a stronger set of letters. This paperwork does not appear any more difficult than filling out the sales contract or mortgage application—yet we fear it because we have never done it.

It should be completely obvious to the tenant that you mean business about collecting rent. From what I understand, the procedure just mentioned solves 99 percent of all late rent problems. Allowing tenants to string you along with nonbinding verbal promises rarely gets the rent paid on time.

Assuming all of the above steps do not get your rent paid—and you are going to court—get an attorney. I have not been through these steps but I have been strongly advised that at this point you get an attorney.

Sixteenth Day of the Month

Assuming everything happened as described and the tenant does not answer the dispossessory warrant, the lawsuit is in default. The court can then grant the landlord a "writ of possession" and the sheriff can remove the tenant immediately. *This is when you go with the sheriff to the house.* He knocks on the door to explain they must move *now*. If no one is there, you give the sheriff a nice comfy chair to sit in while you put the inside belongings out onto the street. The sheriff will watch you—he will not help you. This is when you change the locks. You will want to have a locksmith you can call on short notice. Give the locksmith a heads up that you may need them on a specific day.

DO NOT MAKE THESE LANDLORD MISTAKES

First, I did not come up with these ideas! Actually I do not think I would ever have thought of them. But other landlords have tried these in the past!

- Do not pull the toilets out of the house when the tenant has late payments—you have to keep the house in "habitable" condition.
- Do not remove the front door in winter when the tenant has late payments—see #1.
- Do not change the locks in order to evict the tenant. This only accomplishes getting the people out of the house. Their stuff is still in there, which means you cannot rent it out.
- The three items just mentioned are considered forms of self-help evictions and are illegal under Georgia Landlord Tenant Law. Hopefully, they are illegal in your area, also.
- Do not turn off the tenant's utilities without going through the dispossessory process. You may be subject to a $500 fine.
- This is weird but worth noting—if the rent is paid and the tenant has not been seen for several weeks, you cannot consider the property abandoned.

RESOURCES FOR ADDITIONAL INFORMATION

- On the Web at www.nolo.com
- Your local real estate investors association
- www.carltonsheets.com
- www.money99.com
- www.freeadvice.com
- http://real-estate-law.freeadvice.com/landlord_tenant/
- American Bar Association www.abanet.org/
- A Web page with links to all 50 states' individual bar associations: http://law.freeadvice.com/resources/linkbar.htm

FINAL THOUGHTS FROM THE AUTHOR

I hope you enjoyed this book. It was almost as much labor as the first rental house. You can log on to www.firstrentalhouse.com for links, pictures, and my free newsletter.

MOTIVATIONAL QUOTE

Listen to advice and accept instruction, and in the end you will be wise.

Proverbs 19:20

APPENDIX OF
SELECTED MORTGAGE TERMS

The Internet can provide *pages* of terms! You can find just about anything from www.refdesk.com. While reading an appendix of mortgage terms sounds pretty boring, you might be surprised at what you will learn! Somebody could write a book on just these terms.

adjustable rate mortgage (ARM)   An adjustable rate mortgage is a long-term loan you use to finance a real estate purchase, typically a home. Unlike a fixed-rate mortgage, where the interest rate remains the same for the term of the loan, the interest rate on an ARM is adjusted, or changed, during its term. The initial rate on an ARM is usually lower than the rate on a fixed-rate mortgage for the same term, which means it may be easier to qualify for an ARM. You take the risk, however, that interest rates may rise, increasing the cost of your mortgage. Of course, it is also possible that the rates may drop, decreasing your payments. The rate adjustments, which are based on changes in one of the publicly reported indexes that reflect market interest rates, occur at preset times, typically once a year but sometimes every three, five, or seven years. Typically, rate changes on ARMs are capped both annually and over the term of the loan, which helps protect you in the case of a rapid or sustained increase in market rates. However, certain ARMs allow negative amortization, which means additional interest could accumulate on the outstanding balance if market rates rose higher than the cap. That interest would be due when the loan matured or if you want to prepay.

agreement of sale   A written document in which a purchaser agrees to buy property under certain given conditions, and the seller agrees to sell under certain given conditions. Also known as a sales contract.

alimony   Monthly payments received by an ex-spouse. Payments must be received continuously for three years to be counted toward qualifying income for a loan.

amortization   The process of gradually paying down the principal of the loan. As each payment toward principal is made, the mortgage amount is reduced or amortized by that amount. This is in contrast to an interest-only payment where the principal balance is never reduced. The word *amortize* itself tells the story, since it means, "to bring to death."

annual percentage rate (APR)   The annual cost of a loan, including interest, loan fees, and other costs. A loan's APR is what credit is costing you each year, expressed as a percentage of the loan amount. The APR includes most of a loan's up-front fees as well as the annual interest rate, so it gives a more accurate picture of the cost of borrowing than the interest rate alone. For example, the APR on a car loan or a mortgage, which shows the actual interest you pay, is usually higher than the nominal, or named, rate you are quoted for the loan.

application   A form commonly referred to as a 1003 form, used to apply for a mortgage and to provide information regarding a prospective mortgagor and the proposed security.

appraisal   An estimate of the market value of a piece of real estate made by a competent professional who knows local real estate prices and markets.

assessed value   The value of a property for tax purposes set by a tax assessor according to a formula.

assessments   Special and local taxes imposed upon property that benefits from an improvement that has been made in the vicinity.

asset   Anything of monetary value that is owned by a person. Assets include real property, personal property, and enforceable claims against others including bank accounts, stocks, mutual funds, and so on.

assumable mortgage   A mortgage that can be taken over or "assumed" by the buyer when a home is sold.

balance sheet   A financial statement that shows assets, liabilities, and net worth as of a specific date.

balloon mortgage   The final payment of a balloon mortgage is significantly larger than the payments that are made over the mortgage term. In some cases, the entire principal is due in the balloon payment, with earlier payments having repaid only interest. Buyers might choose a balloon mortgage if they anticipate refinancing at the end of the term, if they will have enough money to pay off the loan in a lump sum, or less wisely if they can afford to buy only because of the comparatively smaller monthly payments that may be available with a balloon mortgage.

basis point   A unit of measure: $1/100$th of one percent. For example, the difference between a 9.0 percent loan and a 9.5 percent loan is 50 basis points.

bill of sale   A written document that serves as evidence of the transfer of title to personal property.

buyer's agent   A buyer's agent represents a buyer in a real estate transaction, negotiating with the seller's agent for a lower price or a contract with more favorable terms. A real estate agent or broker, on the other hand, represents the seller. Although that agent customarily shows the property to prospective buyers, his or her primary obligation is to the seller.

cap A ceiling, or the highest level to which something can go. For example, an interest rate cap limits the amount by which an interest rate can be increased over a specific period of time. A typical cap on an adjustable-rate mortgage (ARM) limits interest rate increases to two percentage points annually and six percentage points over the term of the loan.

capital Any asset that is used to generate income or make a long-term investment. For example, the money you use to buy shares in a mutual fund is considered capital. So is the money you use to make a down payment on a house. Businesses use capital, which is often money from loans or earnings, for reinvestment, expansion, and acquisitions.

capital gains Income from the sale of an asset rather than from the general business activity. Capital gains are generally taxed at a lower rate than ordinary income.

capital improvement Any structure or component erected as a permanent improvement to real property that adds to its value and useful life.

cash reserves Amount in cash after purchase is complete (i.e., after down payment, closing costs, etc.).

cash-out refinance A refinance transaction in which the amount of money received from the new loan exceeds the total of the money needed to repay the existing first mortgage, closing costs, points, and the amount required to satisfy outstanding subordinate mortgage liens. In other words, a refinance transaction in which the borrower receives additional cash that can be used for any purpose.

caveat emptor Latin for "Let the buyer beware." The buyer must examine the goods or property and buy at his or her own risk.

clear title Title not burdened by liens or legal questions.

closing   In real estate, the delivery of a deed, the payment of the purchase price, the signing of notes, and the paying of closing costs, which completes a real estate transaction.

closing costs   The miscellaneous expenses involved in closing a real estate transaction that are over and above the purchase price. Some of the closing costs include title insurance, appraisal fee, and credit report.

closing statement   Also referred to as the HUD-1. The final statement of costs incurred to close a loan or to purchase a home.

combination loan   A loan in which the borrower receives a first mortgage for 80 percent of the loan amount, and a second mortgage at the same time for the remainder of the balance. If the borrower is trying to avoid PMI (mortgage insurance), it is important to consider a combination loan.

combined loan-to-value (CLTV)   The relationship between the unpaid principal balances of all the mortgages on a property (first and second usually) and the property's appraised value (or sales price, if it is lower).

commitment letter   A formal offer by a lender, which states the terms under which it agrees to lend money to a home buyer. Also known as a "loan commitment." This letter will indicate the contingencies that must be cleared prior to funding the loan.

comparables   An abbreviation for "comparable properties;" used for comparative purposes in the appraisal process. Comparables are properties like the property under consideration; they have reasonably the same size, location, and amenities, and have recently been sold. Comparables help the appraiser determine the approximate fair market value of the subject property.

conforming loan   A loan that is eligible for purchase by FNMA or FHLMC. *See* Fannie Mae and Freddie Mac. The current FNMA or FHLMC conforming loan limit is $275,000 and below for a single-family residence, $351,950 and below for a two-unit property, $425,400 and below for a three-unit property, and

$528,700 and below for a four-unit property. Conforming loan limits may change annually. The limit is revised each year according to the change in average sales price of conventionally financed single-family homes.

consumer confidence index   Released each month by the Conference Board, an independent business research organization, the consumer confidence index measures how a representative sample of 5,000 U.S. households feel about the current state of the economy, and what they anticipate the future will bring. The survey focuses specifically on the participants' impressions of business conditions and the job market.

Economic observers and policymakers follow the index because when consumer attitudes are positive—because they think the economy is growing and they have a sense of job security— they are more likely to spend money, which contributes to the very economic growth they anticipate. But if consumers are worried about their jobs, they may spend less, contributing to an economic slowdown.

consumer price index (CPI)   A monthly gauge of inflation that measures changes in the prices of basic goods and services, such as housing, food, clothing, transportation, medical care, and education. Compiled monthly by the U.S. Bureau of Labor Statistics, the CPI—often incorrectly referred to as the cost-of-living index—is used as a benchmark for making adjustments in Social Security payments, wages, pensions, and tax brackets to keep them in tune with the buying power of the dollar.

convertible ARM   An adjustable-rate mortgage (ARM) that can be converted to a fixed-rate mortgage under specified conditions.

credit report   A summary of your financial history, which potential lenders use to help them evaluate whether you are a good credit risk and the likelihood that you will default on a loan. The three major agencies—Experian, Equifax, and TransUnion—collect certain types of information about you, primarily your use of credit and information in the public record, to create these records and sell that information to qualified recipients. You have a right to see your credit history if you have been turned down for a loan. You may also question any information the credit reporting agency has about you and ask that errors be corrected. If the information is not changed following your request, you have the right to attach a comment or explanation, which must be sent out with future reports.

debt-to-income ratio The ratio of a borrower's monthly debt payments to his or her monthly gross income. Lenders use this ratio to determine how much of a loan a borrower is qualified for.

deed A written document that transfers ownership of land or other real estate from the owner, also known as the grantor, to the buyer, or grantee. The form a deed takes varies from place to place, but the overall structure and the provisions it contains are the same. The description of the property being transferred is always included. When you use a mortgage to purchase the property that is being transferred by deed, you may receive the deed at the time of purchase, with the lender holding a lien on the property. Or the deed may belong to the lender until you have paid off the mortgage. In either case, a deed's creation must be witnessed and should be recorded with the appropriate local authority to ensure its validity.

deed of trust The document used in some states instead of a mortgage; title is conveyed to a trustee.

depreciation Certain assets, such as buildings and equipment, depreciate, or decline in value, over time. You can amortize, or write off, the cost of such an asset over its estimated useful life, thereby reducing your taxable income without reducing the cash you have on hand.

discount point Some lenders require you to prepay a portion of the interest due on your mortgage as a condition of approving the loan. They set the amount due at one or more discount points, with each discount point equal to 1 percent of the mortgage loan principal. For instance, if you must pay one point on a $100,000 mortgage, you owe $1,000.

From your perspective, the advantages of paying discount points are that your long-term interest rate is lowered slightly for each point you pay, and prepaid interest is tax deductible. The advantage, from the lender's point of view, is that they collect some of their interest earnings up front.

down payment The percentage of the total cost of real property that you pay in cash as part of a real estate transaction. It's the difference between the selling price and the amount of money you borrow to buy the property. For example, you might make a down payment of $20,000 to buy property selling for $200,000 and take an $180,000 mortgage.

With a conventional mortgage, you are expected to make a down payment of 10 percent to 20 percent. But you may qualify for a mortgage that requires a smaller down payment, perhaps as little as 3 percent. The upside of needing to put down less money up front is that you may be able to buy sooner. But the downside is that your mortgage payments will be larger because you must borrow more.

due-on-sale provision A provision in a mortgage that allows the lender to demand repayment in full if the borrower sells the property that serves as security for the mortgage.

Equal Credit Opportunity Act (ECOA) A federal law that requires lenders and other creditors to make credit equally available without discrimination based on race, color, religion, national origin, age, gender, marital status, or receipt of income from public assistance programs.

equity The value of a property minus outstanding mortgage debt and other liens. Equity is the portion of your property that you have already paid for plus the appreciation, if any, in the value of the property since you acquired it.

escrow account An account held by the lender/servicer, into which a borrower makes monthly installment payments for property taxes, insurance, and special assessments. The lender/servicer disburses these sums as they become due. This type of account is sometimes known as an "impound account."

Fair Credit Reporting Act A consumer protection law that regulates the disclosure of consumer credit reports by consumer/credit reporting agencies and establishes procedures for correcting mistakes on one's credit record.

fair market value The highest price that a buyer, willing but not compelled to buy, would pay, and the lowest a seller, willing but not compelled to sell, would accept.

Fannie Mae A congressionally chartered, shareholder-owned company that is the nation's largest supplier of home mortgage funds. Also known as Federal National Mortgage Association (FNMA). Fannie Mae has a dual role in the U.S. mortgage market. Specifically, the corporation buys mortgages that meet its standards from mortgage lenders around the country and packages those loans as debt securities, which it offers for sale on the open market. By making the money it collects from selling bonds available to lenders, the corporation makes it possible for more potential homeowners to borrow at affordable rates. At the same time, it provides the investment marketplace with interest-paying bonds. Sometimes described as a quasi-government agency because of its special relationship with the federal government, Fannie Mae is a shareholder-owned corporation whose shares trade on the New York Stock Exchange (NYSE).

Fannie Mae's Community Home Buyer's Program An income-based community lending model, under which mortgage insurers and Fannie Mae offer flexible underwriting guidelines to increase a low- or moderate-income family's buying power and to decrease the total amount of cash needed to purchase a home. Borrowers who participate in this model are required to attend prepurchase homebuyer education sessions.

Federal Home Loan Mortgage Corporation (FHLMC) Commonly known as "Freddie Mac," Freddie Mac is a shareholder-owned corporation that was chartered in 1970 to increase the supply of mortgage money that lenders are able to make available to homebuyers. To do its job, Freddie Mac buys mortgages from banks and other lenders, packages them as securities, and sells the securities to investors. The money it raises by selling these bonds pays for purchasing the mortgages. Lenders use the money they realize from selling mortgages to Freddie to make additional loans.

Lenders must be approved in order to participate in the program. Loans must meet Freddie Mac qualifications to be eligible for purchase. To facilitate the lending process, Freddie Mac provides lenders with an automated underwriting tool to help them evaluate mortgage applications.

Freddie Mac guarantees the securities it issues, but the bonds are not federal debts and are not federally guaranteed. Like its sister corporation Fannie Mae, Freddie Mac shares are traded on the New York Stock Exchange (NYSE).

Federal Housing Administration (FHA)   While FHA mortgages resemble conventional mortgages, there are some significant differences. An FHA mortgage is government insured, so lenders are protected against default. The buyer's closing costs are limited, the required down payment is lower, and people who may not qualify for a conventional mortgage because of previous credit problems may qualify for an FHA loan. Further, these mortgages are assumable, which means a new buyer can take over the payments without having to secure a new loan.

There is a price ceiling on the amount a homebuyer can borrow with an FHA mortgage, based on the state and county where the property is located. There are also some expenses, including required mortgage insurance that the borrower must pay.

fixed-rate mortgage   A long-term loan that you use to finance a real estate purchase, typically a home. Your borrowing costs and monthly payments remain the same for the term of the loan, no matter what happens to market interest rates. This predetermined expense is one of a fixed-rate loan's most attractive features, since you always know exactly what your mortgage will cost you.

If interest rates rise, a fixed-rate mortgage works in your favor. But if market rates drop, you have to refinance to get a lower rate and reduce your mortgage costs. Fixed-rate mortgages, which are available in 15-, 20-, and 30-year terms, are more common than adjustable-rate mortgages except in periods when market interest rates are high.

foreclosure A process by which a lender claims title to a mortgaged property, usually because the borrower defaults on the loan or fails to make timely payments on the loan principal and interest. After foreclosure, the lender has the right to sell the property and collect the proceeds of the sale to offset the debt remaining on the mortgage. There is a risk of foreclosure with home equity loans as well as with first and second mortgages.

Most lenders prefer to work with the borrower to avoid foreclosure, if possible, often by extending the term of the loan and reducing the monthly payments.

fully indexed interest rate The sum of the current index rate on an adjustable-rate mortgage (ARM) plus the margin.

good faith estimate A disclosure that must be given to all mortgage loan applicants within three business days of an application. It is an estimate of all settlement charges likely to be incurred at closing.

Government National Mortgage Association (GNMA) Known as Ginnie Mae, the Government National Mortgage Association is an agency of the U.S. Department of Housing and Urban Development (HUD). The agency, backed by the full faith and credit of the U.S. government, guarantees mortgage-backed securities issued by approved private institutions and either insured by the Federal Housing Administration (FHA) or the Rural Housing Service (RHS) or guaranteed by the Department of Veterans Affairs (VA). The agency's dual mission is to provide affordable mortgage funding while creating high-quality investment securities that offer safety, liquidity, and an attractive yield.

Since Ginnie Maes are mortgage securities, they pay interest as well as return of principal with each payment. Ginnie Mae securities are sold in large denominations usually $25,000. But you can buy Ginnie Mae mutual funds, which allow you to invest more modest amounts.

hazard insurance   Insurance protecting against loss to real estate caused by fire, some natural causes, vandalism, and so on, depending upon the terms of the policy.

homeowners insurance   Homeowners insurance protects your investment in your home by promising to repay some or all of the cost of repairing or replacing the home if it is damaged or destroyed. The premium, or bill, you pay for this protection varies based on the value of your home, its location, the extent of the coverage, and the firm providing the insurance. If you have a mortgage on your home, the lender will require that you have at least enough insurance to cover the amount you owe on the loan.

homeowners insurance declaration   A document accompanying a homeowners insurance policy whose purpose is to verify that the homeowners property is, in fact, properly insured.

home equity line of credit   A credit line that is secured by a second deed of trust on a house. Equity lines of credit are revolving accounts that work like a credit card, which can be paid down or charged up for the term of the loan. The minimum payment due each month is interest only.

housing ratio   The ratio of the monthly housing payment in total (PITI—principal, interest, taxes, and insurance) divided by the gross monthly income. This ratio is sometimes referred to as the "top ratio" or "front-end ratio."

HUD   The U.S. Department of Housing and Urban Development.

income property   Real estate developed or improved to produce income. Also referred to as "non-owner occupied property" or "rental property."

index   An economic indicator that lenders use to calculate interest rate adjustments for adjustable-rate mortgages (ARMs). The index used is outside the lender's control.

jumbo mortgage   Also known as a "non-conforming" mortgage. Conventional home mortgages not eligible for sale and delivery to either Fannie Mae (FNMA) or Freddie Mac (FHLMC) because of various reasons, including loan amount, loan characteristics or underwriting guidelines. Nonconforming loans usually incur a rate and origination fee premium.

leverage   An investment technique in which you use a small amount of your own money to make an investment of much larger value. In that way, leverage gives you significant financial power. For example, if you borrow 90 percent of the cost of a home, you are using the leverage to buy a much more expensive property than you could have afforded by paying cash. And if you sell the property for more than you borrowed, the profit is entirely yours.

Loan to Value (LTV)   The ratio of the principal amount of the loan to the lesser of the purchase price of the property or the property's appraised value. You may see this expressed as an 80 percent loan, or 80 percent LTV.

lock-in   The time at which an interest rate is set and the length of time the rate will be held prior to the closing of a loan.

low-documentation   Some loan products require only that applicants state the source of their income without providing supporting documentation such as tax returns.

margin   The amount expressed as a percentage rate that is added to the current index (subject to any rounding rules) in order to determine the interest rate for a loan, subject to a variety of possible adjustments and caps. The margin remains in effect for the life of the loan.

mortgage   A long-term loan used to finance the purchase of real estate. As the borrower, or mortgager, you repay the lender, or mortgagee, the loan principal plus interest, gradually building your equity in the property. While the mortgage is in force, you have the use of the property, but not the title to it. When the loan is repaid in full, the property is yours. But if you default, or fail to repay, the mortgagee can exercise its lien on the property and take possession of it.

mortgage disability insurance   A disability insurance policy, which will pay the monthly mortgage payment in the event of a covered disability of an insured borrower for a specified period of time.

mortgage insurance (MI)   Also known as "private mortgage insurance" (PMI). Insurance which protects mortgage lenders against loss in the event of default by the borrower.

non-conforming loan   Also known as a "jumbo mortgage." Conventional home mortgages not eligible for sale and delivery to either Fannie Mae (FNMA) or Freddie Mac (FHLMC) because of various reasons, including loan amount, loan characteristics, or underwriting guidelines. Nonconforming loans usually incur a rate and origination fee premium.

non-owner occupant   A borrower who will not be residing in the subject property as their principal residence; the borrower on rental/investment property.

note   A written promise to repay a loan. It includes the loan amount, interest rate, and term.

origination fee   A fee imposed by a lender to cover the administrative costs of setting up a mortgage. This will include the preparation of documents and certain processing expenses in connection with making a real estate loan. This is usually charged as a percentage of the amount loaned, such as one point or one percent.

payment table   In the table principal and interest payments are rounded up to the next dollar. Shown is a 30-year fixed-rate mortgage loan. Note that taxes and insurance would have to be added to these payments. (Most mortgage company websites have a calculator that can provide specific payment information on your situation.)

Loan Amount

Interest Rate	$50,000	$75,000	$100,000	$125,000	$150,000
6.50%	$317	$475	$633	$ 791	$ 949
7.00%	$333	$499	$666	$ 832	$ 998
7.25%	$342	$512	$683	$ 853	$1,024
7.50%	$350	$525	$700	$ 875	$1,050
7.75%	$359	$538	$717	$ 896	$1,075
8.00%	$367	$551	$734	$ 918	$1,101
8.25%	$376	$564	$752	$ 940	$1,127
8.50%	$385	$577	$769	$ 962	$1,154
8.75%	$394	$591	$787	$ 984	$1,181
9.00%	$403	$604	$805	$1,006	$1,207
9.25%	$412	$617	$823	$1,029	$1,234
9.50%	$421	$631	$841	$1,052	$1,262
9.75%	$430	$645	$860	$1,074	$1,289
10.00%	$439	$659	$878	$1,097	$1,317

Variation: For an $88,000 loan at 8% take the payment for the $100,000 loan and multiply by .88. Example: $734 × .88 = $646.

PITI Principal, interest, taxes, and insurance—the components of a monthly mortgage payment.

preapproval A process that mortgage lenders use to determine how much money they would lend you based on a thorough review of your financial situation. Lenders issue a preapproval letter, which strengthens your position when bidding on a home, as it shows sellers that you will be able to raise funds needed to purchase.

prepaids   Those expenses of property which are paid in advance of their due date and will usually be prorated upon sale, such as taxes, insurance, rent, and so on.

prepayment clause   A clause that stipulates the amount of principal a borrower may prepay ahead of schedule without penalty as well as the prepayment penalty for larger prepayments.

prepayment penalty   A charge a borrower pays to prepay a loan before it is due. Not allowed for FHA or VA loans.

prime rate   This typically refers to the best rate for short-term commercial paper. This is not a stable index.

private mortgage insurance (PMI)   Insurance coverage obtained from mortgage insurance companies to protect lenders against risk of making higher loan-to-value loans. Typically required on all first mortgages with an LTV that exceeds 80 percent. The borrower usually pays the PMI premiums.

rate lock-in   A written agreement in which the lender guarantees the borrower a specified interest rate, provided the loan closes within a set period of time.

refinancing   Taking out a new loan to pay off an existing mortgage. This is done to obtain a lower interest rate or to borrow cash on the equity in a property that has built up on a loan.

reverse mortgage   A loan, available to homeowners over 62, that lets you convert your equity in your home into cash. Banks and other financial institutions lend you a designated amount of money—usually paid to you in installments or available as a revolving line of credit—based on a percentage of your home's market value, your age, the interest rate, and the fees associated with arranging the reverse mortgage.

You do not have to make any loan repayments while your reverse mortgage is in effect. The loan comes due when you die or when the home is no longer your principal residence. In most cases, the lender takes over the home, which is generally sold to repay the loan.

sales contract　A written document in which a purchaser agrees to buy property under certain given conditions, and the seller agrees to sell under certain given conditions. Also known as an "agreement of sale."

second mortgage　A mortgage that ranks after a first mortgage in priority. If the loan is not repaid, the first mortgage holder has first right to the property; the second mortgage holder receives anything remaining.

seller carry back　An agreement in which the owner of a property provides financing, often in combination with an assumed mortgage.

teaser rate　A low introductory interest rate on a credit card or an adjustable rate mortgage (ARM). The lender must tell you how long the teaser rate lasts and what the real cost of borrowing will be at the end of the introductory period.

title insurance　The insurance that protects the lender and if an owner's policy is purchased, the homeowner, against loss resulting from any inconsistencies in the title of a property from liens or other title problems relating to a property.

total debt ratio　Monthly debt and housing payments divided by gross monthly income. Also known as "obligations-to-income ratio" or "back-end ratio."

Truth-in-Lending Act　Also known as "Regulation Z." A federal law requiring a disclosure of credit terms using a standard format. This is intended to facilitate comparisons between the lending terms of different financial institutions.

underwriting   The analysis of risk involved in making a mortgage loan to determine whether the risk is acceptable to the lender. Underwriting involves evaluating the property as outlined in the appraisal report, and also evaluating the borrower's ability and willingness to repay the loan.

unsecured personal loan   A loan that is not backed by collateral.

BIBLIOGRAPHY

Adams, John. *The Landlord's Survival Guide*. Decatur, GA: John Adams, 2000.

Adams, John. *The Top Ten Mistakes That Landlords Make*. Decatur, GA: John Adams, 2000.

Allen, Robert G. *Nothing Down*. New York: Simon & Schuster, 1984.

Allen, Robert G. *The Challenge*. New York: Simon & Schuster, 1987.

Allen, Robert G. *Multiple Streams of Income*. Hoboken, NJ: John Wiley & Sons, 2002.

Dyer, Dr. Wayne. *Transformation: You'll See It When You Believe It*. New York: W. Morrow, 1989.

Fannie Mae. *Becoming a Landlord by Fannie Mae*. Available through the Consumer Resource Center, 800-732-6643, Washington, DC: 1994.

Guzik, Ron. *The Inner Game of Entrepreneuring*. Chicago, IL: Upstart Publishing Co., 1999.

Hopkins, Tom. Edited by Warren Jamison. *How to Master the Art of Selling*. Scottsdale, AZ: Champion Press, 1980.

BIBLIOGRAPHY

Kiyosaki, Robert. *Rich Dad, Poor Dad*. New York: Doubleday, 1999.

Kiyosaki, Robert. *Retire Young, Retire Rich*. New York: Warner Books, 2002.

Lovenheim, Peter. *How to Mediate Your Dispute*. Berkeley, CA: Nolo Press, 1996.

Portman, Attorney Janet, Marcia Stewart, and Attorney Ralph Warner. *Every Landlord's Legal Guide*. Berkeley, CA: Nolo Press, 2002.

Stewart, Marcia, Attorney Ralph Warner, and Attorney Janet Portman. *Leases and Rental Agreements*. Berkeley, CA: Nolo Press, 1996.

Many of these books can be purchased by logging on to my web site www.firstrentalhouse.com.

INDEX

Access, Section 8 housing standards, 70
Accountant, functions of, 32, 43, 112–113
Accounting procedures, 112–113
Adams, John, 32, 35, 168, 172–173
Adjustable rate mortgage (ARM) loans:
    characteristics of, 27–28, 203–204
    fully indexed interest rate, 213
    index, 215
    teaser rates, 219
Advertising, 87, 153–154, 183, 191
Affirmations, 59–60
Agreement of sale, 204. *See also* Sales
    contract
Air conditioners, 90–91
Air quality, Section 8 housing standards,
    69–70, 91
Alimony, 204
Allen, Robert G., 29, 36
Aluminum siding, 89–90
America Community Bankers Association,
    26
American Association of Small Property
    Owners, 47
American Gas Association (AGA), 68
Amortization, 204
Annual Escrow Statement, 131
Annual percentage rate (APR), 204
Appliances, 90, 94
Appraisals, 119, 125, 193, 205
Appreciation, 16, 53
Assessed value, 205
Assessments, 205

Asset, defined, 205
Assumable mortgage, 205
Attorney, functions of, 32, 41–42

Back-end ratio, 219
Backyards, 146, 163
Balance sheet, 205
Balconies, safety issues, 69. *See also*
    Porches
Balloon mortgage loans, 28, 118–121, 205
Bank loan, opportunity analysis, 85
Bankruptcy, 25, 151
Basis, 184
Basis point, 205
Becoming a Landlord by Fannie Mae, 46
Bedrooms, Section 8 housing standards,
    66–67
Bill of sale, 205
Blackwell, Tommy, 38–40, 191
Blue-collar workers, profile of, 166
Business cards, 114
Business entity, 112
Business leads, sources of, 41–42
Business referral networking groups, 58
Buyer's agent, 205–206

Cap, 206
Capital, defined, 206. *See also* Working
    capital
Capital expenditures, 184
Capital gains, 9, 16, 184, 206
Capital improvements, 206

Carbon monoxide, 94
Carpet cleaning, 88
Carter, Jimmy and Rosalyn, 56
Cash back at closing, 5
Cash flow, 53
Cash Flow 101 game, 34–35, 61
Cash-flow opportunity analysis:
    advertising costs, 87
    bank loan, 85
    equity line, 84–85
    exterior/interior considerations, 89–90
    homeowners insurance, 86
    maintenance costs, 88
    mortgage insurance, 87
    rehab costs, 88–89
    taxes, 85–86
    total payment, 87
    vacancy factor, 87–88
    worksheet, 84
Cash-out refinance, 206
Cash reserves, 19, 206
Caveat emptor, 206
Certificates of deposit (CDs), 15–16
Certified public accountant (CPA), functions
    of, 32, 43, 112–113
Challenge, The (Allen), 29, 36
Chamber of commerce, as information
    resource, 58
Circuit breaker inspections, 69
Civic organizations, as information resource,
    58
Clear title, 206
Closing, defined, 207
Closing attorneys, 42, 193
Closing costs, 119, 122–123, 207
Closing date, 193
Closing process:
    participants in, 127–128
    RESPA required disclosures, 131
Closing statement, 207
Coaching, 13
Code violations, 51
Collateral, 18–19
Collections, rental payments:
    procedures, 101–102, 165
    timely, 197–198
Combination loan, 117, 207
Combined loan-to-value (CLTV), 207
Commercial banks, as financial resource,
    17
Commitment letter, 207
Community Bankers Association, 37
Community Bankers Association of Georgia,
    26, 37
Community banks, 37, 120
Comparables, defined, 207
Complaints, dealing with, 111

Computer software, accounting programs,
    113, 187
Condominiums, 76, 83, 95
Conforming loan, 207–208
Consumer confidence index, 208
Consumer Credit Counseling Services, 24
Consumer price index (CPI), 208
Contractors:
    dealing with, 32, 43, 46
    insurance coverage, 45
    repeat service, 45
    selection factors, 44–45
    sources of, 44–46
Convertible ARM, 208
Convertible mortgage loans, 28
Credit applications, 156–158
Credit cards, 12, 21–22, 25
Credit checks/credit references, 100–101,
    151–152, 163–166
Credit counseling services, 25
Credit improvement strategies, 24–25
Credit problems:
    bad credit, 29
    types of, 24
Credit repair clinics/services, 25–26
Credit reporting agencies, 22–24
Credit reports:
    defined, 208–209
    importance of, 19–20, 29, 163–166
Credit score, 18, 20–22, 25
Credit unions, as financial resource, 18
Cremens, Jill, 26, 115–116
Criticism, dealing with, 13

Daily challenge, 54–56
Damaged property, security deposit and, 104
Deal killers, 163
Debt consolidation, 26
Debt elimination, 25
Debt-to-income ratio, 209
Decks, safety issues, 92, 96, 103
Deed, 209
Deed of trust, 209
Default, 216
Demand notice, 199
Department of Community Affairs (DCA), 63,
    70, 72
Department of Housing and Urban
    Development (HUD):
    development of, 64
    functions of, 65, 71, 213–214
    landlord responsibilities, 71–73
    rental payments, 64–66, 76–77
    RESPA, 129
    Section 8 housing Basic Standards, 66–71
Department of Veterans Affairs (VA), 213,
    218

Index

Depreciation, 9, 53, 209
Discount points, 123, 209–210
Discrimination, 107–108
Dispossessory warrant, 199–200
Dispute resolution, 104–105
Dividend income, 9
Divorce, economic impact, 83, 151, 165
Divorced dads, renter profile, 167–168
Doors, safety issues, 93
Down payment, 5, 18, 65, 82, 210
Drainage:
  problems with, 94
  Section 8 housing standards, 70
Driveways, 90
Due-on-sale provision, 210
Dumpsters, sources of, 147
Duplex units, 51
Dyer, Dr. Wayne, 32, 35–36

Earned income, 9
Economic conditions, as motivation, 7–9
Electrical system:
  faulty wiring, 94
  Section 8 housing standards, 68–69
Emotional obstacles, getting over, 52,
  186–187
Environmental hazards, 70, 103–104
Equal Credit Opportunity Act (ECOA), 210
Equifax, 20–24, 208
Equity, defined, 210
Equity line of credit, 12, 56, 82, 84–85,
  116–118, 121–122, 124, 190
Escalation clause, 174
Escrow account:
  defined, 210–211
  RESPA required disclosures, 131
Every Landlord's Legal Guide
  (Portman/Stewart/Warner), 47, 105, 176
Eviction:
  dispute resolution, 104
  information resources, 202
  landlord mistakes with, 201
  process overview, 174–202
  security deposits, 109–110
Expenditures, types of, 113, 183–184
Experian, 20, 23–24, 208
Exterior conditions, 89–90, 93
Exterminators, 102

Failure:
  cost of, 54
  fear of, 53–54
Fair Credit Reporting Act, 211
Fair Housing Act/Fair Housing Amendments
  Act, 107–108
Fair market value, 211
Family size, Section 8 housing vouchers, 68

Fannie Mae (FNMA):
  characteristics of, generally, 17–18, 26,
    152, 190–191, 207, 211
  Community Home Buyer's Program, 211
  defined, 215–216
Fear, getting over, 10, 52, 181–182
Federal Home Loan Bank Board, 27
Federal Home Loan Mortgage Corporation
  (FHLMC), 211–212
Federal Housing Administration (FHA), 129,
  212–213, 218
Financial goals, importance of, 7–8, 25
Financial reserves, 12–13
Financial resources, case illustration:
  balloon loan, 118–121
  equity line of credit, 117–118, 121–122,
    124, 190
  fixed-rate mortgage, 122
  refinance, 121–122
Financial resources, types of, 16–19, 82. See
  also Financial resources, case illustration
Financial security, 3
5 Attitudes Toward Rejection, 53–54
Fixed-rate mortgage loans, 27, 122, 212–213
Flipping, 112
Flooring, 69
Food preparation area, Section 8 housing
  standards, 67
Foreclosed houses, 36, 39, 95–96, 190
Foreclosure:
  defined, 213
  rates, 78
  specialists, 39
Foundations, 90
Freddie Mac (FHLMC):
  characteristics of, 17–18, 26, 152, 207
  defined, 215–216
Freedom Builders, 42
Front-end ratio, 214
Fully indexed interest rate, 213
Furnace, 68, 91, 94
Furnished homes, 83

Garages, 95
GaREIA (Georgia Real Estate Investors
  Association), 18
Georgia Landlord Tenant Law, 201
Get-rich-quick schemes, 10
GFCI (ground fault circuit interrupter) outlets,
  69
Ginnie Mae, 214
Good faith estimate, 213
Good Faith Estimate (GFE), 130
Government, rental payments from, see
  Section 8 housing
Government National Mortgage Association
  (GNMA), 213. See also Ginnie Mae

INDEX

Guardrails, 69
Gutters, 92
Guzik, Ron, 59–60

Habitat for Humanity, 55–56
Handrails, 69, 103
Hard money lenders, 18–19
Hazard insurance, 214
Heinsite Services, 100, 164
Home equity, as financial resource, 9
Home equity line of credit, 214
Homeowners association (HOA), 76, 81
Homeowners insurance:
    declaration, 214
    defined, 214
    significance of, 86, 214
Homestead exemption, 86
Homework, importance of, 77
Hopkins, Tom, 53
House Price Index, 9
Housing Assistance Payments (HAP)
    contract, 72
Housing ratio, 214
Housing structure/materials, Section 8
    housing standards, 69
How to Master the Art of Selling (Hopkins),
    53
*How to Mediate Your Dispute: Find a Solution
    Quickly & Cheaply Outside the
    Courtroom* (Lovenheim), 105
HUD house, 97
HUD-1 Settlement Statement, 130–131, 193
HVAC (heating, venting, air-conditioning),
    93–94

Income property, defined, 215
Incorporation, 112–113
Index, 215
Infomercials, Carlton Sheets, 1, 6, 29, 33
Information resources, 29, 46–47, 53
Initial Escrow Statement, 131
Inner Game of Entrepreneuring, The (Guzik),
    59–60
Inspections:
    components of, 92–94
    importance of, 51, 91–92
    legal issues, 101
    move-in, 169, 175–176
    opportunity analysis, 89
    property, 173–174
    Section 8 housing, 71–72
    tenant qualification process, 169
Insurance coverage:
    hazard, 214
    homeowners, 86, 214
    importance of, 11, 45
    in lease agreements, 175

legal requirements, 101
mortgage, 87
mortgage disability insurance, 216
private mortgage insurance (PMI), 87,
    123–124, 216, 218
renters, 86, 101, 175
Interest rate(s):
    economic impact of, 8, 18, 78
    lock-in, 215, 218
    lock preapproval, 29
Interior conditions, 89–90
Intimidation, dealing with, 52, 54–55
Investment goals, 53
Investor success factors, 10–14

Job security, 8
Johnson, Skip, 44
Judgments, 25, 165
Jumbo mortgage, 215

Keipper, Phil, 3
Killer lease, 172
Kitchens, Section 8 housing standards,
    67–68
Kiwanis, 58
Kiyosaki, Robert, 32–35, 75
Knowledge, importance of, 52–53

Landlord, generally:
    expectations, 181–182
    mistakes made by, 201
Landlord's Survival Guide, The (Adams), 35,
    172
Landlord-tenant relationship, 176–177
Landscaping, 146
Late fees, 109
Late notice, 198–199
Late payments, credit scores and, 21
La Tip, 42
Lead-Sharing Club, 42
Learning curve, 53
Lease, *see* Lease agreements
    breaking, 107
    contract terms, 101, 105–106
    rental agreement compared with, 106
    Section 8 housing, 71–72
    terms of, 105–107
Lease agreements:
    early termination, 175
    effective, 171–172
    escalation clause, 174
    eviction process, 174
    front page, 172
    insurance coverage, 175
    landlord-tenant codes, 177–179
    liability issues, 174
    move-in inspection, 175–176

Index

property inspections, 173–174
property use and maintenance, 173
rent, 172–173
resources for, 176–179
Lease/purchase, 151–152, 166
Lease Writer (Portman/Stewart/Warner),
176
Leases and Rental Agreements
(Stewart/Warner/Portman), 112
Legal considerations:
collections, 101–102
credit checks/credit references, 100–101
discrimination, 107–108
dispute resolution, 104–105
environmental hazards, 103–104
information resources, 105, 112
leases, 105–109
liability, 102–103, 110–111
maintenance, 102
management supervision, 104
rental agreements, 105–109
safety liability, 102–103
security deposits, 101–102, 109–110
tenancy contract terms, 101
tenant privacy, 103
Lender-borrower relationship, 28–29
Leverage, 215
Liability issues, 43, 86, 102–103, 110–111,
174
Liens, 25, 165
Lighting:
safety issues, 103, 146
Section 8 housing standards, 68–69
Limited liability corporation (LLC), 43,
112
Litigation:
avoidance strategies, 111–112
personal injury, 111
Small Claims court, 104
Loan-to-value (LTV) ratio, 18, 118–119,
215, 218
Location:
analysis guidelines, 79–82
importance of, 11, 50, 78–79, 96
Lock-in, 215
Lovenheim, Peter, 105
Low-ball offers, 98, 184
Low-documentation, 215
Low-income housing, 64
Lyden, Sean, 42

Maintenance, generally:
contract terms, 102, 111, 173
costs, 88
fees, 76
Manufactured houses, 96–97
Margin, 215

Marketing, 152–154
Market value, 77, 82
Masonry, 93
Medical bankruptcy, 151
Mentors:
benefits of, 187
functions of, 57–58
relationship with, 57–58
sources of, generally, 56–58
types of, 32–37
Mistakes:
dealing with, 13, 31, 33–34, 182–183
by landlord, 201
Mortgage(s):
defined, 216
disability insurance, 216
insurance (MI), 87, 216
loan application, *see* Mortgage application
terminology, 203–220
Mortgage application:
defined, 204
documentation requirements, 116–117
process overview, 28–29
RESPA required disclosures, 129–130
Mortgage bankers:
as financial resource, 17, 32, 37–38
as information resource, 58
Mortgage Bankers Association of America,
17
Mortgage brokers, functions of, 26, 115–116
Mortgage lenders:
functions of, 26, 32, 37–38
meeting with, 28–29
mortgage loans, types of, 26–28
Mortgage loans:
applications, *see* Mortgage application
types of, generally, 26–28
Mortgage note, 17
Mortgage Servicing Disclosure Statement,
130
Motivational tape programs, 32–33, 35, 53
Multiple Streams of Income (Allen), 29, 36
Multiunit projects, 50, 83

National Credit Union Administration, 18
National Foundation for Credit Counseling,
24
National Real Estate Investors Association,
47
Negative cash flow, 10
Negligence, 110
Negotiations, 184–185
Neighborhood:
location analysis, 79
Section 8 housing standards, 70
New South Federal Savings Bank, 119
Non-conforming loan, 216

Nondealer house, 112
Non-owner occupant, 216
No-pets clause, 107
Note, 216
Nothing Down (Allen), 3, 36

Obligations-to-income ratio, 219
Opportunity mentality, 12
Optimist International, 58
Origination fee, 216
Owner financing, 17–18, 51

Paint/painting:
　costs, 88
　home inspections, 93
　lead-based, 70, 104
　maintenance, 91
　selection factors, 88
Partnerships, as financial resource, 13, 18
Passive income, 9
Payment, *see* Rental payments
　opportunity analysis, 87
　table, 216–217
Personal bankruptcy, 25
Personal injury lawsuits, 111
Pest control, 175
Pets, 107
Piggyback loan, 117
PITI (principal, interest, taxes, and insurance), 214, 217
Plan implementation:
　affirmations, 59–60
　case illustration, 49–52
　continuous learning, 52–53, 55–56
　daily challenge, 54–56
　failure, fear of, 53–54
　fears, overcoming, 52
　mentors, sources for, 56–59
Playgrounds, location analysis, 80
Plumbing, home inspections, 92–93
Points, 123
Porches, safety issues, 69, 95
Portman, Janet, 105, 112, 176
Positive attitude, importance of, 59–60
Powercore, 42
Power of attorney, 127
Preapproval, mortgage loans, 28–29, 38, 116, 124, 190, 217–218
Prepaids, 218
Prepayment clause, 218
Prepayment penalty, 218
Pressure washing, 90
Prime rate, 218
Privacy rights, 103
Private investors, as financial resource, 18

Private mortgage insurance (PMI), 87, 123–124, 216, 218
Project team:
　accountants, 32, 43
　attorneys, 32, 41–42
　contractors, 32, 43–46
　mentors, 32–37, 56–59
　mortgage banker, 32, 37–38
　mortgage lender, 32, 37–38
　real estate agent, 32, 38–41
Property devaluation, 11
Property maintenance, 64
Property management:
　functions of, 52
　supervision of, 104
Property taxes, 43, 80–81
Purchaser, defined, 127

Quadruplex unit, 50, 52
QuickBooks, 113, 187

Ranges, electric *vs.* gas, 90
Rate lock-in, 218
Rate of return, 15–16
Real estate agents:
　foreclosure specialists, 39
　functions of, 32, 38–41, 128
　selection factors, 41
Real estate investment club, 18, 58
Real Estate Settlement Procedures Act (RESPA), 127–129
Recreational areas, location analysis, 80
Referrals, subcontractors, 146–148
Refinance/refinancing, 121–122, 125, 218
Regulation Z, 219
Rehab:
　benefits of, 88–89
　case illustration, 134–144
　cost-effective tips, 145–149
　process guidelines, 144–145
　project evaluation, 133–134
Rent:
　demand notice, 199
　escalation clause, 174
　late notice, 198–199
　lease agreement, 173
Rental agreements, 105–109
Rental payments:
　contract terms, 108–109
　Section 8 housing, 76–77
Rental rates, location analysis, 80
Renter profiles, 166–168
Renters insurance, 86, 101, 175

Index

Repair schedule:
  contract terms, 111
  Section 8 housing, 72
  time factor, 185–186
RESPA required disclosures:
  Annual Escrow Statement, 131
  HUD-1 Settlement Statement, 130–131
  Initial Escrow Statement, 131
  loan application, 129–130
  Servicing Transfer Statement, 132
Retire Young, Retire Rich (Kiyosaki), 33, 53, 75
Reverse mortgage, 218–219
Reviewing property, 183, 191–192
Rich Dad, Poor Dad (Kiyosaki), 33, 156
Risk tolerance, 33–34
Roadways, location analysis, 80
Rodent infestation, 70–71, 102
Roof structure, 69, 91–92
Rotary, 58
Rural Housing Service (RHS), 213

Safety liability, 102–103, 112
Sales contract, 119, 125, 192, 219
Sanitary facilities, Section 8 housing standards, 67
Savings accounts, 12, 25
Savings and loans, as financial resource, 16–17
School system, location analysis, 79
S corporation, 112
Second mortgage, 219
Section 8 housing:
  amount of rental payments, 76–77
  benefits of, 63
  how it works, 64–66
  information resources, 73
  landlord responsibilities, 71–73
  participation in, 71
  structural qualifications, 66–71
Security deposits:
  characteristics of, 101–102, 109–110, 176
  Section 8 housing, 65–66, 71
Security system, 103
Self-motivation, 2
Seller, defined, 128
Seller carry back, 219
Seminars, benefits of, 53, 194–195
Septic systems, 81, 90
Servicing Transfer Statement, 132
Sheets, Carlton, 32–33, 145
Showing the house, 155–157
Siding, maintenance and repair, 89–91
Signature loans, 19
Single-family houses, 50, 76, 83, 162

Single mom, renter profile, 167
Size of house, importance of, 83
Small claims court, 104
Smoke detectors, 68
Stairways, 69
Stewart, Marcia, 105, 176
Structural damage, 93
Subcontractors:
  payment schedule, 148–149
  selection factors, 146–148
  working with, case illustration, 135–138
Support group, 7
Support services, location analysis, 79
Swimming pools, 146, 190

Taxes, opportunity analysis, 85–86
Tax incentives, 9
Teaser rate, 219
Tenancy contract terms, 101, 105–106
Tenant(s):
  complaints from, 111
  credit checks/credit references, 100–101
  criminal background check, 100, 159
  privacy rights, 103
  qualifying, 161–169
Tenant qualifications:
  credit check, 163–166
  red flags, 162–163
  renter profiles, 166–168
  verifying funds, 168
Tenant search:
  case illustration, 157–159, 194
  credit applications, 156–158
  prequalification process, 154
  verifying funds, 168
Termites, 96
Thermal environment, Section 8 housing standards, 68
Thrift institutions, 16
Time investment, 2, 11, 183, 185–186
Timeline, case illustration, 189–195
Title insurance, 219
Top ratio, 214
Top Ten Mistakes That Landlords Make, The (Adams), 35, 168
Top to Bottom Services, 44
Total debt ratio, 219
Trade lines, defined, 164
Transformation: You'll See It When You Believe It (Dyer), 35–36
TransUnion, 20, 23, 208
Treasury bill yield, 27–28
Triplex units, 52
Trump, Donald, 53
Truth-in-Lending Act, 219

INDEX

Underwriting, 220
Unsecured personal loan, 220
U.S. Federal Trade Commission, 26
Utilities:
   location analysis, 81
   opportunity analysis, 90

Vacancy, 87–88
Ventilation, maintenance and repair, 94
Verifying funds, 168
Vermin infestation, 70–71
Volunteer work, 55
Vouchers, Section 8 housing, 64–65

Warner, Ralph, 105, 176
Warranties, 95

Water heaters, 91
Water supply:
   inspection of, 92
   Section 8 housing standards,
      70
Wealth creation, 53, 186
Weather stripping, 93
Web sites, lease agreements,
   176–177
Windows, 93
Wood infestation, 193
Working capital, 116
Write-offs, 9
Writ of possession, 201

Ziglar, Zig, 12